AF406279

"The Ultimate Warning from Jesus Christ"

Table of Contents

The LORD saw how great the wickedness of the human race had become on the earth, and that every inclination of the thoughts of the human heart was only evil all the time. The LORD regretted that he had made human beings on the earth, and his heart was deeply troubled.

Philippians 1

For I want you to understand what really matters, so that you may live pure and blameless lives until the day of Christ's return.

My fascination with Biblical prophecy began shortly after surrendering my life to Christ as a young man. After my redemption, I began to search the scripture deeply for answers on why my generation and our nation were uniquely straying so far from God. I began to realize that Christ was protecting my life, and my search for truth even before my personal encounter with Him. During this time, I remember as a teen, a Time Magazine titled, "Is God Dead?" coming to our door that shook me to the core. My journey for the answers to my purpose in life and my despair surfaced quickly as I slid badly into the late "Sixties." As the darkness increased, so did the turmoil in my soul. It made me realize that God was not dead, but he seemed dead to me. This began my personal descent with the generations following.

This past year, Time Magazine released an identical background cover except the title declared, "Is Truth Dead?" It was a gruesome reminder of my original quest for answers. The content of this issue was frightening and blasphemous as a hypocritical mandate that could not have been further from the truth. It testified the tragic mantra that "all things are relative and subjected to our personal perception." We have witnessed the reversal of our nation being baptized into an amoral global deluge. It has replaced the eternal vision and truth of the scripture with humanist engineering through our socialist media. The radical shift on how we think, and relate to one another encircles us back to the beginning of the greatest rebellion of mankind upon the earth. We are now repeating the history from the Days of Noah.

I have spent most of my life as a pastor and a chaplain to lost and hurting incarcerated kids that have suffered from a myriad of painful trials, many with no father, no spiritual heritage, and trapped by a reversed moral compass. The most tragic thing has been witnessing the continuing demise of our nation where the birth pains that Christ warned us would lead us into the seven final years of deadly consequences. As we chose to lock God out of our government, our educational system and our devotion, it slowly destroyed the fabric of our culture and the original foundatio of our nation. We now witness it daily, if not hourly through the distorted media and the techno-explosion that enslaves us.

There are countless things we can put our finger on to define where we are in the last days concerning planet earth and the imminent return of Jesus Christ. The grave question that many are asking today is devolving as we witness a profound "great falling away" from the faith to the consummation of lawlessness. We are now witnessing the final count of Biblical prophecies being fulfilled, but we will now focus on what Jesus said about it.

As we repeat the history of the former generation of Noah, we have also forgotten God as the nation has hurled itself into a sensual carnival with a tragic addiction for more. Violence, technology, and corruption induced by humanity's marriage with the dark forces of angelic evil once again distort all humanity into living for the moment, divorced from God. The same bell of history is now tolling the epic warning for us today as it rang for Noah's generation that was entombed in the spiritual waters spewed from the Prince of darkness.

✎ Chapter One ✎

Treading the Waters of this World

1 Thessalonians 2

Don't you remember that when I was with you, I used to tell you these things? And now you know what is holding him back, so that he may be revealed at the proper time. For the secret power of lawlessness is already at work; but the one who now holds it back will continue to do so till he is taken out of the way. And then the lawless one will be revealed, whom the Lord Jesus will overthrow with the breath of his mouth and destroy by the splendor of his coming.

Something went fatally wrong after the world wars that ravaged the nations as it brought global fatigue fading into apathy as the prophesized Mystery of Lawlessness exploded. In the same hour, the miracle of the rebirth of Israel drew the spiritual lines forming on Israel's hope for the future. The decade of the Fifties had caused great compromise and a hunger for the material things of this world created from the technology from the wars. This opened the door to the spell from Noah's day that enslaved the globe as the consent to "selfism" leavened the concurring generations.

The era of the Sixties brought an unprecedented, worldwide revolt against all things godly, and even many who claimed to be Christian were caught in the web. Our nation then began to follow Europe into this mystery of "selfism" that began to ferment and bring a global world order to bring false peace on the surface. But it was truly about "the New World Order" that Adolph Hitler longed for as he titled his book with this same title. This eventually brings the Antichrist from behind the curtain laboring to finish the systematized error that is against anything reverent. This rebirth of the Way of Cain is manifesting through this false progressive mixture of economics, politics and spirituality from the deception from the very beginning.

The presence of the Holy Spirit through the "restrainer" is right now confining the revelation of the Man of Lawlessness, the Antichrist, and the Spirit of Lawlessness that is fully at work in the children of disobedience. This spell is getting full traction in seizing global reign, and we are witnessing this desperate change right before our eyes. The coming Antichrist will soon lead the descent into the clutches of evil and he will set the global web of depravity. The enormity of the acts of past moral monsters as the Caesars, Stalin, and Hitler, pale in comparison to the coming evil one as the Mystery of Lawlessness empowers and enlivens him. This is the sorcerous wave of delusion that Jesus warned us about that would hasten His return.

The fingerprints from the Days of Noah involved four types of grave iniquities: great wickedness, evil imaginations of every kind, extreme violence, and total corruption. It is bewildering that these things are the primal leavening process in the foundation of today's society, causing an eclipse of temporal madness as in the generation of Noah. Today, our children are now taught from kindergarten to adulthood through every branch of the media, and the educational system, that the world is a selfish carnival with no eternal purpose, just carnal pleasure. Even the spiritual high ground that the church once rested upon, now lies beneath the same spiritual waters that once covered the earth in the Days of Noah. The eternal hope of the Gospel has been drowned in temporal indulgence with no regard for why we were even created, even in the nominal church.

These errors have enveloped this world in a sensual cloud as an eclipse from any truth that would penetrate. It is about a total forgetfulness of God and the disregard of His will. By removing Christ as the Center, it has rendered the masses upon earth so selfish that it has the world presently filled with lewdness, injustice, oppression, and violence. In Genesis Six, the Lord warned that "My spirit shall not always strive with man." God continues to give us every chance to turn to Him and to turn away from sin, but if we choose to arrogantly ignore the prophetic warning, His Spirit will soon be withdrawn and the Day of Judgment will come upon us without awakening. The world is full of people who continue in their worldly lives as if nothing is happening. We must look deep into the heart of Jesus as He compels us concerning the history of Noah and the age that was swept away by the waters of sovereign judgment.

In every age, the Lord always calls out a true witness. The Great Flood was preceded by four generations of prophets and preachers to warn of the coming judgment. The ten generations from Adam to Noah's generation reflect God's forbearance in holding back judgment in the hope that mankind would repent. There was a remnant from Noah's line that held their faith in this perilous time. Genesis Four and Five are very important, because it provides the Messianic genealogy, the line of blessing and the line of Noah to the coming deluge. It is also the only authentic history from the creation to the next monumental event of the flood. This remnant spoke for God like Enoch, as the salt of the earth at that time.

God's imminent coming destruction of the people at that time restrained the disposition of these men until they too give way to evil. It was not merely because those who did not believe in God were morally corrupt, evil and licentious. They claimed they still believed in God, even those who once made offerings to God, no longer feared God and had no place for God in their hearts. Everything they began to do went against God's requirements and they followed along with the torrential course of the age. The entire world had become saturated by evil and degenerate to the point that God didn't bear to even look upon them. But even so, humanity at that time had absolutely no desire for repentance. We must solemnly look at today as the repeat of this age without a clue. Our time truly fulfills the words that Franklin Roosevelt. He spoke "this generation has a rendezvous with destiny." This generation is stepping into an even greater destiny.

The Critical Warning from Jesus

Luke 17

Just as it was in the days of Noah, so also will it be in the days of the Son of Man. People were eating, drinking, marrying and being given in marriage up to the day Noah entered the ark. Then the flood came and destroyed them all.

At the coming betrayal leading to the cross, the disciples knew that Christ was about to be crucified and exit to heaven, leaving them alone, vulnerable to the forces of evil. The disciples of Jesus panicked that they were about to lose Him to death as they desperately asked him what to do with a sobering question, "What will be the imminent sign of your return?" Jesus made it very clear that it would be a time beyond their present sphere and to be to the final generation with a tragic deficit. As perilous as their situation was, Jesus had to sober them up from believing that they were going to be rescued from the hands of the Romans and the Pharisees at that time. Yet, after His resurrection, Jesus spent a month giving them a clear mission to embrace that would bring the Gospel of His cross to the ends of the earth.

The line was drawn in the sand of Eden with the first proclamation of the coming Reddeemer. After the seduction in the garden, this birthed a full-fledged invasion by Satan, the Prince of this World, and his conspiring myriad of fallen Watchers. This had left the globe in a spiritual eclipse beyond the pale of darkness. As the Lord spoke, "there was evil upon man's heart continually." This was the twisted campaign from the first angelic rebellion with its invasion to thwart God's new creation and to hijack it into his delusive submission.

In the Days of Noah, the invasion of earth had been blatantly scarred with a rebellion in every imaginable way in betraying the Lord. Every element of this systematized error that is known today as the new world order was birthed from this point in Genesis. Cities and secular godless empires, weaponry and war, sensual culture, music and the arts and all things that were possible alienated mankind from their loving Lord. These were all laced into the generation of Noah's society by the invasive hellish sorcery by the army of fallen angels cast from heaven.

As they viewed themselves as progressive and cultured, God wept over their vile condition. Three times the text repeats that the earth was corrupt, meaning "morally degraded." The Hebrew word "corrupt" means destructive. Twice it is said that the earth was filled with violence. Moral degradation and violence always go together. When people cast off God's standards for right and wrong, self-intent becomes the standard. Selfishness possessed whatever it could harness. Violence was the gruesome result, because of the degree of moral degradation and violence, the earth became a living hell.

Jesus' explicit point by His urgent prophecy was that this same arena of sin and rebellion will again shake the entire globe again in the same way right before His return. The global apostasy that Jesus forecast is now deluging the planet as people are intoxicated from a life alienated from eternal validity. The Apostle Paul revealed this same mandate in the Book of Second Thessalonians where we are warned that the Antichrist appears authoring the final rebellion known as the "Mystery of Lawlessness" which is an extension of the "Way of Cain."

There are many lessons taught by the Old Testament concerning Noah and Lot. Both men lived among wicked men obsessed by their own pleasure and both men were taken from God's judgment, which was poured out upon the rest. In both cases, no one seemed aware that the judgment of God was coming until it was too late. Jesus warned it would also the same as in the days of Lot by saying "People were eating and drinking, buying and selling, planting and building. But the day Lot left Sodom, fire and sulfur rained down from heaven and destroyed them all. "It is interesting that the people of the day were exceedingly wicked, yet Jesus did not emphasize it.

The answer is quite clearly suggested by the Lord's description of the activities they were engaged in at the time judgment fell upon the unsuspecting people. Everybody was going about their daily activities of living. People were eating and drinking, marrying, and giving in marriage, buying, and selling, planting, and building. It was "life as usual" for these people when the end came. They never realized that judgment was coming upon them because they lived for the moment. True idolatry is worshipping things above God. Life to them consisted of worldly pleasure caught up in the pursuit of the sensual, alienated from God and denying spiritual truth.

The Indictment in this Book

Matthew 16

He replied, "When evening comes, you say, "It will be fair weather, for the sky is red, "and in the morning, "Today it will be stormy, for the sky is red and overcast." You know how to interpret the appearance of the sky, but you cannot interpret the signs of the times.

The purpose of this book is to provide the collective exposure of the final rebellion that has weaved through the ages leading to the final return of the Messiah. It is an indictment that is unquestionable in the light of God's Spirit and God's Word. The definition of an indictment is a formal charge or accusation of a serious crime. Something that serves to illustrate that a system or situation is fatally flawed. This indictment was embedded from the very beginning with the godless seed of rebellion in the Book of Genesis. As we are now encompassed in the culmination of these seeds of apostasy, the remnant is looking up for the imminent return of the Deliverer.

Jesus told us two basic scenarios that would be engraved in the generation that He would return to. The first was the equation of blindness with the Days of Noah and the second was the blurring sin that occurred in the Days of Lot. The core of Sodom's day was the other warning that they were obsessed with daily life, money, sexual sin, and no room for repentance. These signs are magnified in every way in our present generation. I cannot describe the severe importance that we understand why Jesus was so intense about the warning of the Days of Noah and Sodom. It is sad how deceptive and glamorous that sin can appear and how quickly it can strike like a viper. The keys to our prodigal planet are written from the pages of Genesis to the Book of Revelation. The principalities and powers of the "fallen ones' continue to deluge the earth with the hidden leaven of their "secret knowledge' that deceives humanity on the despair of chasing the wind.

I remember years ago when Wendy's had a commercial with a little lady looking at this huge hamburger bun with this tiny piece of hamburger and she says, "Where's the beef?" When I visit many churches today, I ask the same question, "Where's the beef?". The response is too often, "stop rocking the boat!" The truth is that neither Noah nor Jesus had any notion to keep the peace or worry about rocking the boat. They functioned through obedience to the Holy Spirit and the love of Christ. Jesus said that offenses must come and that they would be expensive. This was right at the point that John the Baptist lost his head for standing against the Pharisees and the Romans.

Facing the Final Impending Storm

1 Peter 1

Therefore, with minds that are alert and fully sober, set your hope on the grace to be brought to you when Jesus Christ is revealed at his coming.

In this final hour of trial, it is far more critical and relevant to this year, to this very day and to this very minute to understand the advent of Christ's return and its comparison to the generation of Noah. Jesus did not want anyone to be ignorant and deceived concerning His second return. He warned us to "be ready, because the Son of Man will come at an hour when you do not expect him."

One of the main cautions that Jesus gave the disciples about the Days of Noah and Lot was the instant judgment visited on their rebellious generation without any warning. Jesus pointed out that, although the people of Noah's day were totally depraved, they were not the least bit concerned about it. They were carrying on the events of their lives without a single thought of the judgment of God knocking upon their door. Repenting was the last thing on their mind and heart. Apathy is so rampant today, along with an addiction for the temporal. May God turn our hearts back to Him and train us to "fight the good fight."

Even with all the signs of the last days, the world continues as if nothing is out of the ordinary. This is just what the people in Noah's day did before the flood came and swept them all away. And Jesus says this is exactly what we should expect to see before the Rapture. All the signs of Christ's returning to set up His Millennial Kingdom are present in this generation. This book will sum up the imminent apostasy that swept away the generation of Noah as it is rushing torrent compelling us into the cataclysmic Great Tribulation.

The Fall of

HUMANITY

ETERNAL LIFE	DEATH'S RULE
INNOCENCE	SINFULNESS
GODLY NATURE	FALLEN NATURE
GODLY REIGN	MAN'S REBELLION
MAN'S PURPOSE	HOPELESSNESS
GOD'S IMAGE	IMAGE OF THE BEAST
MAN'S PURPOSE	MAN'S PURPOSE

The Redemption from the of

MESSIAH

FORGIVENESS
ETERNAL IFE RETURNS
REBORN NATURE
CHRIST RULES
GODLY IMAGE
GOD'S IMAGE
PEACE & PURPOSE

❧ Chapter Two ❧

The Daze of Noah

Genesis 6

The LORD saw how great the wickedness of the human race had become on the earth, and that every inclination of the thoughts of the human heart was only evil all the time. The LORD regretted that he had made human beings on the earth, and his heart was deeply troubled. So, the LORD said, "I will wipe from the face of the earth the human race I have created and with them the animals, the birds, and the creatures that move along the ground, for I regret that I have made them." But Noah found favor in the eyes of the LORD.

With the flashing and rumbling sky, Noah looked over the dark and electric horizon with horrific pain to realize that no one was repenting from the hideous rebellion that had seduced his entire culture. After suffering a hundred and twenty years of appealing to his unbelieving generation to repent, not a soul had found their way to their knees except for the family of Noah. The dark stain upon the planet eclipsed the Light from every other soul as man consented to live under the perverse spell of the fallen ones and their seductive reign of terror.

All of Noah's pleas had fallen on ears that were deaf from the roar of an indulgent age that had abandoned God and His eternal will. What was it that was so deceptive and alluring that it could have swept away an entire generation with absolutely no regard for life's intent? It was rooted from the same selfish pride that had eroded the prince of darkness from his first estate at the throne of God. Through the encrypted darkness, Noah felt God's broken heart from seeing man's appetite from carnal addiction and devotion to evil that had replaced his simple and pure devotion to their Creator.

From the arrogant parade led by Satan, humanity marched in step blindly and began to worship at the altar of a dark sensual and demonic world. The guilt from Eden and the loss of true spiritual identity, left humanity completely open for attack from the invasion. Any trace of innocence had vanished as they hurled themselves into the arms of the cruel villainous fallen ones. At this time, they were left with no resistance from sin. The ways once learned by Adam as he walked the paths of Eden had been replaced with the desire for what looked good, tasted good and whatever pleased the senses. Carnality and blind ambition erased God from their memory as they fell deeply into an affair with the evil Prince and their own evil desire. The sorcery of "selfism" stained the planet and impaled darkness into the hearts of men.

The initial fallout from heaven by these angelic rebels termed the watchers that had brought them to earth to extend their betrayal. They assaulted God's new creature through the wayward Way of Cain to establish a foothold for their continuous betrayal. They riddled the unseen world with the dark lord's evil devices and secret sorceries. These angelic rebels began to roam the earth like scavengers spreading their ministry of dissension and betrayal to finally commit the unthinkable. From Eden, the raging course of the age of Noah swept away any basic acknowledgement or worship of God and any accountability to their Creator, except for the protected line of Noah.

Their wicked planned deception brought agony upon Noah and his family as they were exposed to the torrid rebellion of that fatal day. The evil days of Noah's generation was intended to be rescued through Noah and his family through their premier devotion to divine command. Noah spent over a century building this massive ship in the middle of the desert. Surely the favorite sport of the day was taking a flask of wine up on the hill and throwing verbal stones at this apparent radical extremist. The Lord once again revealed His great patience as He waited for Noah to complete his mission.

Noah's generation was so deceived that they counted the thought absurd that God would hold them accountable for anything or to bring judgment. As today, God's patience was misunderstood to be a tolerance for sin. The masses asked, "Where is this God that looms over the horizon?" In a brief time, man had vacated God from their minds, their communities, and their culture with an arrogant ignorance. Within ten generations, the planet became unrecognizable from the sinful implosion and their carnal knowledge. The greatest travesty is this generation turned to worship of the surrounding devilish angels and the works of their own hands. This horrific paradox is followed today by the worship of our own idolatry as we crush the heart of God.

Each generation has the choice to let their natural inclination repeat the cycle or to find a better way. The magnitude of Noah's generation coming right after the fall of humanity accelerated everything. People lived much longer in the era before the flood as they accumulated the degenerative effects of the fall because the environment in the pre-flood world was so tainted with the blanketing vapor of evil encircling the globe. This began the cycle of generational sin of disobeying God's will by sinning against the one law given to Adam. These sins involve behavioral patterns and ways of thinking that keep us trapped in the past.

The flood baptized the planet to eradicate the hideous rebellion that saturated that generation. As Noah found favor and grace in the eyes of the Lord, he also found isolation and pain. Noah suffered greatly through building the ark and the persecution he received from the godless clan of unbelievers. Noah was gracefully separated from his generation by his faith, his Lord, his obedience, and his mission. It surely had been a protection for him. It kept him from being vexed by the spell of ungodliness that had encircled the planet not only saved his household, but he brought the judgment from God upon that unrepentant generation. The mission of Noah, like many, would not end well until he reached the gates of heaven.

The Daze over the Generation of Noah

1 Peter 3

After being made alive, he went and made a proclamation to the imprisoned spirits, to those who were disobedient long ago when God waited patiently in the days of Noah while the ark was being built. In it only a few people, eight in all, were saved through water.

The daze that overwhelmed Noah's worn face spoke volumes on the gravity of this insipid rebellion. We will delve a great deal into the moral, spiritual, and intellectual collapse of Noah's day as we proceed. Apathy, selfishness, and a thirst for the forbidden had spread like wildfire through the descendants of Cain as they seeded the earth with a godless system of empiricism, idolatry, weaponry, and technology inspired by the unfaithful angels.

Cain's murderous heart and angelic collusion spread throughout the planet with an arrogant disregard for what he spawned upon his own companions. It is amazing how quickly Satan began to twist God's image into the prideful, selfish image of himself. He had stolen man's domain and brought the battle for earth under his attack. The blessing of "free choice" was the vehicle that Satan employed to distort man's image and human will through his lethal temptation.

The growing rebellion leading the assault on mankind led into hands of the fallen angels that had spun a web of secret knowledge from the thread of "the forbidden tree of Eden." The veiled angelic conspirators merchandised their implosive "selfism" that had been seeded in the Garden of Eden. Conviction from sin was replaced with an amoral thirst that nothing was illegal or toxic. The great delusion of Hedonism created a total disregard for the sin that once crouched at the door of Cain now leavened the entire civilization. The Way of Cain then spread like a cancer engulfing the masses in the toxic sorcery that he was so solemnly warned about. Most believers today do not begin to understand the prolific influence of the plot of the Way of Cain on Noah's generation, and how it is coming to its final fruition now in this present evil age. The sin from Eden followed the first lawless murderer, Cain. He became the co-author with the invading Prince of this World to continue his assault from Eden.

The Overwhelming Foothold of Evil

2 Corinthians 2

In order that Satan might not outwit us. For we are not unaware of his schemes.

There are strategies to warfare that are so critical in beginning a campaign of assault. The invasion of Normandy was the most critical decision of World War Two. Without a foothold there in Europe, we had no way to enter the heart of the battle. Two things were pertinent according to General Eisenhower. Secrecy and deception were invaluable to make it successful. This was not a unique strategy, but a necessary one. My father was a part of this great invasion that turned the tide in World War Two. My dad landed on the beaches in Normandy where we lost over ten thousand men in one morning. The price that was paid by families were unbearable but without this invasion the Nazis would not have been contained and the Nazis would have won the war. Breaking through the barriers was critical in establishing the ground assault that led to breaking the back of their resistance.

Satan has a myriad of deficits but stupidity is not one of them. The Prince of Darkness found the foothold that he was looking for to launch his second attack on the globe. His initial act was his original seduction of Eve by his cunning deception. He hid in the skin of the most beautiful animal of the field so that she would have no suspicion. He then deceived and separated her from her Creator and even her unsuspecting husband. The serpent established the stronghold of communication that selfish desire was the core of existence and meaning.

Cain brought the second stronghold from his arrogant independence from God and His will. It culminated in then the murder of Abel as the second lethal marker as Satan crouched at the door with the harness of murder. This was provoked by the sin of pride that exploded into rage and jealousy as Cain's sacrifice was rejected by God and Abel's was accepted. His arrogant response was "Am I my brother's keeper?" There was not an ounce of remorse. The hardened heart of Cain gave Satan the foothold to launch the extended invasioof the angelic rebellion that had poisoned the first family.

The Rabid Culture of Noah's Generation

When tempted, no one should say, "God is tempting me." For God cannot be tempted by evil, nor does he tempt anyone, but each person is tempted when they are dragged away by their own evil desire and enticed. Then, after desire has conceived, it gives birth to sin; and sin, when it is full-grown, gives birth to death.

The deep settled rebellion of "selfism" was first magnified on the earth through the residing culture in the Days of Noah. Satan was enthused by his strategy from the Garden of Eden, but it was only the launching pad for what his true intention and schemes were to be. It was to continue his tactic of putting "self "on the throne and to rule and reign through deception by twisting man to think it was his idea. The worship of selfism was at an epic proportion and the masses didn't care where it originated. They thought they were living normal lives during the time Noah lived, just before the Flood. They were oblivious to the impending disaster. They really didn't care as they continued to live their lives the way they pleased. They ignored God, and the longer they persisted, the more unsound their reasoning became and the harder it became for them to change. God's image in humanity had been scarred beyond recognition.

After the flood, it became evident that even within the family of Noah, unbelief and selfism was abiding within the first family. When God had commanded Noah's descendants to "be fruitful, to multiply, and replenish the earth" as with Noah, instead they took up their permanent residence, with no apparent intention to spread out and recover the earth. With this attitude, the seed of rebellion revived as the culture from the flood took root with Nimrod at the Tower of Babel. They sought a name for themselves rather than to honor the name of their Creator, who is above all and whose name is worthy of all praise. The Lord was left with no choice but to confound their language to disrupt and disburse them. Mankind's rebellion in culture came full circle again. The people earned a name for their city, but not a name of their own choosing. Their city's name became Babel, from a related word meaning "confusion.

⁰⁹ Chapter Three ⁰⁹

The Flood and the Calling of Noah

1 Peter 2

For if God did not spare angels when they sinned, but sent them to hell, putting them in chains of darkness to be held for judgment; if he did not spare the ancient world when he brought the flood on its ungodly people but protected Noah, a preacher of righteousness, and seven others; if he condemned the cities of Sodom and Gomorrah by burning them to ashes, and made them an example of what is going to happen to the ungodly.

God calls us to obedience, even when it does not make sense. Some Bible scholars claim that it had never rained until Noah's flood. This is mainly a silent argument which assumes that water came up as mist from the ground. It's not important if it had never rained anywhere before, or if Noah lived in the desert. God's call to Noah to build the ark seemed almost beyond absurd. The idea that God would send such an overwhelming flood that all life would be destroyed seemed incomprehensible. God's instructions must have sounded even more unbelievable to him. There have been a few times when God calls me to do something, and it didn't make any sense. We walk by faith, but we cannot see how God will make any sense out of the situation He is calling us into. When you find that God is calling you to do something, just do it.

The term "microcosm" from the Greek "mikros kosmos" means little world and designates the individual as being a "little world" in the expansive universe. The whole of a complex structure of creation was contrasted with Noah's life and calling, becoming the only representative left for God upon the earth. After the fall of Adam from not protecting and representing the Lord, Cain stepped with a hellish conspiracy with the fallen angels. The Lord had no choice, but to raise up Noah, a microscopic light in a dark world.

The heart and soul of this grim cataclysm was about salvation, not destruction. It was about reconstructing the future through cleansing and setting boundaries between humanity and the evil renegade fallen angels that brought the fallen ways to the new creation of Adam. This is about the revelation that this cataclysmic setting that would be set right at the eventual coming of the Messiah. The tragic beginning would eventually be eclipsed by Another.

This pathway started in Genesis as a definition to help validate the history of Noah and the flood, and to consummate in the Book of Revelation. Sadly, there are many who have discarded the truth of Noah and the ark as a fable, or a metaphor at best. It is imperative that we deal with the historical data of the flood, not just the Biblical account. There is probably more skepticism about the Noachian flood than any portrayal in the scripture, except for Jonah. It is often written off as a good bedtime story, yet it is laced in almost every historical national library of the early ages.

The history of the Great Flood is not only recorded in the Bible, but myriads of stories are verified in texts from around the world. Later, we will mention a long list of the documents of a deluge that floods the skepticism of the unbelieving world. We will go in to detail later what transpired with this evil generation concerning the fallen angels. It is one of the deepest mysteries in the Word of God. The revelation of the deluge of Noah's day is profoundly important, and it is at the heart of Christ's empowering warning to us concerning the Days of Noah. It is a unique warning, specifically to this faithless generation that has every earmark of the days of Noah and Sodom. The epic story of Noah should be shouted from the rooftop, or we will continue in ignorance and apathy, missing the mark of having a sense of urgency concerning the coming of Christ.

The idea that one man and his family created a ship large enough to save an entire remnant of animals from the globe is often considered laughable, unless you explore the background with the invention of technology and its intervention in the beginning. To erect such a massive ship and to provide the needs for the living creatures would have required a huge effort of epic proportion. If you exclude the impact of the fallen angels with technology, it seems even more absurd. This explains the elevated level of technology which we will cover in the future chapters concerning the source of "secret knowledge." God speaks so many times in the scripture, "what the enemy meant for evil, the Lord meant for good.

The evidence of the Great Deluge is found laced in historical legends, traditions, and writings. Practically all ancients have legends and accounts that their ancestors survived a great flood. The similarities of the records cannot possibly be coincidental. The combined evidence of these legends corroborates the Bible's ancient testimony that all humans have descended as the survivors of a flood that destroyed the world of mankind but those upon the ark. These legends have a global span because this was a global flood to eradicate the lawless acts and spells of the fallen angels that had immersed the entire planet in their rebellion and sorcery. As mentioned, it is amazing to see the recorded impact of the flood upon the writings in human history, yet there is such ignorance and rejection to treat the deluge as mythic. The enemy does anything to expel or deny the impact of our Creator upon His creation. Satan has been the dispenser of the "Great Lie" from the very beginning. The Days of Noah reveal his ultimate goal to divest humanity of his loyalty to the Lord.

The Biblical Depiction of the Flood

Genesis 6:13

God said to Noah, "I am going to put an end to all people, for the earth is filled with violence because of them. I am surely going to destroy both them and the earth.

According to Judaism, as expressed in the Talmud, the first five books of the Old Testament, Noah was a tremendous example of standing against the tide of an unbelieving age and evoking the great hope of righteousness and salvation that comes through obedience to God. In a world riddled with sin and unbelief, Noah patiently built an ark to spare his family and those who would repent from the tide of judgment that would devour the earth.

Other Writings on the Great Flood

Noah is even considered a highly important figure in Islam and is seen as one of the most significant prophets of all. The Quran contains forty-three references to Noah. Noah's narratives largely consist around his preaching as well the story of the Great Flood. The Quran focuses on several instances from Noah's life more than others, and one of the most significant events is the Great Deluge. Unfortunately, Islam always misses God as many of the Jewish faith. It is like they are on the outside looking in because they are. Without Christ's revelation, there is only a shadow. Reading the Book of Job gives the carnal perspective of Job's friends and then God speaks out of the storm. Without God's true input from the present storm, there is no true perspective.

The Genesis narrative is prevalent on all the continents, and among almost all peoples of the earth, flood accounts have been found. According to scientist Dr. Duane Gish, there are more than 270 stories about a catastrophic flood from cultures around the world. Most of these stories bear similarities to the biblical story of Noah and the ark. These accounts all refer to a destructive flood occurring early in the respective tribal histories.

In each case one or a few individuals were saved and were charged with repopulating the earth. Anthropologists have collected approximately three hundred flood stories. Original stories of a global flood reside in almost every nation of the earth. Early missionaries were amazed at discovering isolated tribes and areas that had inherited stories with incredible similarities to the Biblical accounts of a worldwide deluge.

Ancient civilizations from China, Babylon, the Soviet areas, Africa, India, America, Hawaii, Scandinavia, and Polynesia all have their detailed histories of the giant deluge. These accounts describe the warnings of the dark generation of Noah, the building of a vessel before the flood, and the saving of the animals of the earth. The consistency of these writings has been discovered all over the globe. When the Bible and the Babylonian accounts are compared, there are great similarities discovered that leave no doubt these stories are rooted in the same global catastrophe. The expanse of historic materials shows the same tragedy of this terrible rebellion.

The Global Flood

I am surely going to destroy both them and the earth.

The Depth and Duration of the Flood.

Noah's Ark is said to have come to rest on the mountains of Ararat.

Researchers now believe they've found evidence of human activity near the boat shaped formation in the mountains. Today's mountains in the Ararat region include Mount Ararat which rises to 17,000 feet in elevation.

The Physical Causes for the Flood.

The Bible explains that the breaking open of "all the fountains of the great deep" and the "windows of heaven" were the primary causes. The "deep" is the ocean; thus the "great deep" could hardly be the cause of a limited local flood. The "windows" seem to refer to the waters above the atmospheric firmament. These were global causes, producing a global effect.

The Need for an Ark.

Noah was given many years of warning, long enough to walk anywhere on earth. The animals also would have lived globally and so could have migrated anywhere. There was no need for an Ark if the flood was local. The Ark's size, big enough to carry two or seven for some of each land dwelling animal, testifies of a global flood. Building such a huge ship for a local flood for which there was ample warning would be ludicrous.

Destruction of All Mankind.

The flood's primary purpose was to cleanse sinful mankind. While the earth's preflood population is not given, reasonable assumptions based on Biblical data for average family size, life spans, and age of parent at time of first born yield a population far in excess of the maximum Mesopotamian population.

Varying Flood Legends from Around the World

And now, it is because of my hope in what God has promised our ancestors that I am on trial today.

Mesopotamia

The story of Noah may be part of the Abrahamic canon, but the legend of the Great Flood almost certainly has prebiblical origins, rooted in the ancient civilizations of Mesopotamia. The Sumerian Epic of Gilgamesh is thought to be perhaps the oldest written tale on.

Africa - Southwest Tanzania

This is an excerpt from African lore. Once upon a time the rivers began to flood. The god told two people to get into a ship. He told them to take lots of seed and to take lots of animals. The water of the flood eventually covered the mountains, then finally the flood stopped.

Asia China

A Chinese classic called the Hiking, talks about a family that was saved from a great flood. This ancient story tells that the entire land was flooded; the mountains and everything, however one family survived in a boat. The Chinese consider this man the father of their civilization.

Babylon

There was an old man named Utnapishtim, who told the following story. The gods came to Utnapishtim to warn him about a terrible flood that was coming. They instructed Utnapishtim to destroy his house and build a large ship.

Chaldea

The god Chronos warned Xuthus of a coming flood and told him to build a boat. In this ship Xisuthrus was to put his family, friends and two of each animal. The flood came. When the waters started to recede, he let some birds loose. They came back and he noticed they had mud on their feet.

As mythic Zeus witnessed the earth getting worse, Zeus decided that he would destroy all humans. Before he did this, Prometheus, the creator of humans, warned his human son Deucalion and his wife, Pyrrha. Prometheus then placed this couple in a large wooden chest. The rains started and lasted until the whole world was flooded.

They Blinded Me with Science

"Science without religion is lame; religion without science is blind."   Albert Einstein

Hebrews 11

Now, faith is confidence in what we hope for and assurance about what we do not see. This is what the ancients were commended for. By faith, we understand that the universe was formed at God's command so that what is seen is not made out of what is visible.

There is a new poll released shows that young adults in particular, belief in God is plummeting. This research assumes the primary driver behind a loss of faith among young people is the church's rejection of science, which is naive and foolish. To put it bluntly: young people aren't leaving the faith because of science, they're leaving because this generation has chosen unbelief and "selfism" as its platform from the sins of the father.

Creationism and the study of evolution has been a controversial debate for decades now, leaving many people on one side or the other. Creationism argues that faith should take precedent over science, basing its beliefs on one book for premier guidance, the Bible. Evolutionists believe that the earth is much older than the Bible describes, and that plants, animals, and humans are a result of a natural progression called evolution.

They claim there were no common ancestors from whom we came, that it was a natural selection process, stemming from inorganic compounds and nature. For many people in the scientific world, it is hard to take a stance on this issue since there is limited evidence of evolution, but that is where faith in God and what God has done comes into effect. According to a great medieval philosopher, Moses Maimonides, "conflicts between science and the Bible arise from either a lack of scientific knowledge or a defective understanding of the Bible." This involves an issue that would distract from the mission of this book if we took the needed space.

It is understood that the earth is governed by specific "laws of nature" that have been discovered through experimentation and scientific observation. These laws and principles were designed and established by the order of the God of our universe. The confirmation of these laws and properties of the universe is the very basis of good science. This was the attitude of almost all scientists until the late eighteenth century. At this time, many scientists also began to theorize that the earth's lifespan was far longer.

During the Age of Enlightenment, significant works were created to excuse natural causes for the miracles recounted in the Bible. This short period has brought great confusion and some ridiculous speculation to derail the thought of intelligent design and an Eternal Creator with a presiding purpose. We are now seeing a revival with many in the scientific world because there is no answer for there not being an intelligent designer and the ability to create something from nothing. If there was a "big bang," I would like to know who provided the fuel.

It is fascinating how faith is defamed as being gullible when the thought of no intelligent designer is the height of absurdity. Common sense is evidence enough to eradicate the truth that nothing can author life itself. The modern science of geology was founded in Europe during the eighteenth century. New scientists sought to understand the history and shaping of the earth through the physical evidence found in and minerals. Many early geologists were believers that preferably sought to link the geological history with that in the Bible.

The Faithful Line of Noah

Hebrews 11

By faith Noah, being warned of God of things not seen yet, moved with fear, prepared an ark to the saving of his house; by which he condemned the world, and became heir of the righteousness which is by faith.

Noah descended from the faithful line of Abel and Enoch. The eternal reason for this was to tutor him on how to serve God. Abel, the son of Adam, was a simple shepherd who always offered the Lord the firstborn of his flock. The meaning of the name Abel was "breathing spirit." Abel brought life to the promise of a coming Redeemer. Finally, Abel's blood greater thins and affirmed his great faith by the greatest sacrifice.

Enoch, before his rapture had the testimony that he walked with God for three centuries. His relationship was so intimate with God that he was taken away from the earth to heaven. Enoch didn't witness the flood, nor did he hear the wailing of those who were swept away by the waters of judgment. Enoch as the first rapture, was delivered from the harvest of wrath which followed the universal godlessness of humanity. It was not his to fight the battle of righteousness to the bitter end; but by a secret rapture he avoided death.

Noah learned to stand his ground and built an ark of mercy and salvation. His faith demonstrated both the judgment and the salvation of God. God's true righteousness demands the retribution for sin, but his mercy almost always leaves a door open for an escape. The deluge was a horrific account of justice but also a glorifying example of redemption. Noah was mocked and called a fool, but he stood in the gap for God's will.

The legacy of the line of Noah split tragically between faith and unbelief with his sons. Shem, the son of Noah continued the way of Abel. Noah's son Ham, continued the Way of Cain leading to Nimrod and the Tower of Babel. The order of Noah's descendants was paramount in the future of mankind after the flood.

Noah's Mystery of Righteousness by Faith

By faith, Noah, when warned about things not yet seen, in holy fear, built an ark to save his family. By his faith he condemned the world and became heir of the righteousness that is in keeping with faith.

Righteousness is mentioned over two hundred times in the Bible yet the way of righteousness is mysterious, especially in the Old Testament. The truth of God is often veiled. Only the Holy Spirit can truly reveal it. The knowledge of God is free to all, but the revelatory knowledge of God is hidden or veiled until the veil is removed by the Holy Spirit. We who are of the faith may say, "I was once blind, but now I see."

The Bible is the story of how God is constantly reclaiming the earth and restoring humanity. The term dispensation refers to the ages that would transpire in the history of humanity through time leading to eternity. God's plan of redemption was to be in Noah with his heart of faith preparing the way with a time table for his actions. We are told that Noah was a righteous man, blameless in his generation, and that he walked with God.

Noah's Vision

Genesis 5

He named him Noah and said, "He will comfort us in the labor and painful toil of our hands caused by the ground the Lord has cursed."

Noah's vision came to him through the eyes of God's grace. As the world looked through selfish eyes of desire, Noah fixed his heart on God's purpose and the need for a perishing generation. Noah had a spiritual vision that governed his life. His obedience and passion for God was the driving force behind his mission. There was a sobering understanding that he had a century to accomplish the enormous task of building a ship to hold the seed of hope for the coming age. His commitment and patient endurance spoke volumes to an age engulfed in perversion and lawlessness that refused to listen to the truth from God.

Noah had been bruised by the callousness of the age. Noah was the first in the line of prophets to follow and warn man of the coming judgments upon the apostasy of the times. Those who bore God's image had broken God's heart, leaving Noah to stand in the gap to save the remnant of his family lineage and testify the validity of the coming deluge. Noah clung to the grace the Lord had bestowed upon him as he watched the day of retribution approaching. Noah's vision kept him from being entangled in the web of indulgence. His life was cradled in the unfailing grace of God in a moment of judgment. He was cleansed by the conviction and the reverent fear of God.

The Mission of Noah

Genesis 6

So, God said to Noah, "I am going to put an end to all people, for the earth is filled with violence because of them. I am surely going to destroy both them and the earth. So, make yourself an ark of cypress wood; make rooms in it and coat it with pitch inside and out.

Noah's mission was to rescue the creatures of the earth through the coming flood and to reestablish the covenant between God and man. Noah's mission was given directly from the Lord with a detailed blueprint on how to build the ark. What a solemn mission Noah had received from the hand of God that this would bring the outpouring of wrath upon his community and the whole world. Over the years he must have become overwhelmed by the callousness of the heart of man to mock the oncoming judgment and to ignore the warnings of Noah and his family.

Noah, the Prophet

Hebrews 11

By faith Noah, when warned about things not yet seen, in holy fear built an ark to save his family. By his faith he condemned the world and became heir of the righteousness that comes by faith.

Noah was the first prophet. A prophet is always one who proclaims the Word of the Lord, and who sometimes predicts the future. Noah was a prophet in both senses. The Book of Genesis doesn't lay much stress on his "prophetic ministry," but Peter calls him a "herald of righteousness." The office of prophet has become tainted by false prophets and aimless meandering about the temporal. The prophet's vocation is not to tickle ears or pat backs, but to call people to holiness, which requires repentance and obedience. Noah also predicted the future in two different ways. The first way is obvious: He predicted the coming world-wide judgment of God. The second way is not so obvious: His very name predicted the coming rest for the people of God, which is the definition of his name.

Noah, the Evangelistic Preacher

Genesis 6

Now the earth was corrupt in God's sight and was full of violence. God saw how corrupt the earth had become, for all the people on earth had corrupted their ways. So, God said to Noah, "I am going to put an end to all people, for the earth is filled with violence because of them.

One of Noah's toughest ministries is that of being an evangelist. He was the first evangelist ever mentioned in the Bible. Noah is described as a "preacher of righteousness." In what way was he a preacher? The Greek word "kerux" refers to a herald, or "one who announces." Reaching out for over a century and not having one response had to be pure agony. Even though they did not receive the message, Noah was God's means of getting the warning to those who needed it.

The tradition shows Noah giving both a warning and a means of salvation. Noah pleaded for people to repent, which would certainly fit with his own source of salvation. Noah was truly the first evangelist of finality. Today's evangelist, although they have the vast advantage of the whole counsel of Bible prophecy, they face the same hardness of heart as in the Days of Noah. Since the wrath of God is one of the main foundations of today's word, how can we escape to preach it?

Chapter Four

The Returning Spiritual Deluge

Jeremiah 2

Your wickedness will punish you; your backsliding will rebuke you. Consider then and realize how evil and bitter it is for you when you forsake the Lord your God and have no awe of me," declares the Lord, the Lord Almighty.

Have you ever felt alone in a meaningless universe, unable to bear going through the motions, having no sense of direction, and feeling like you have lost all hope? You could be going through an eclipse of the soul. To a person who has bought into the regular motions of modern society, life can seem like it is a joke on autopilot; guided by ego and hiding in habitual sensuality from a tragic wound. These next two chapters are a blueprint of what is happening to this generation. It is so critical that we understand the connection that Jesus gave to this present evil age and the Days of Noah.

After the waters had receded, the impact upon the earth must have been horrific. Noah surely was in shock at the incredible impact that waters had bestowed upon the land. It must have sunk in the magnitude of what God was forced to do try to stop the deep spiritual inquisition by Cain and the fallen angels. The landscape must have been unrecognizable from the days before the flood. Noah stepped into the forbidding earth with desperation over what is next. The animals and plants from the previous world were buried under hundreds of feet of sand and mud.

The eternal purpose of God to save men from themselves was in God's heart long before the Days of Noah. The mandate of God's purpose to save humanity had entered at the fall of Adam as the confirmation of God's love and purpose in history would be a long road of recovery. The covenant of God expressed by the rainbow was initiated after the sacrifice offered up by Noah when they had finally landed. This covenant was initiated and dictated by God. While some ancient covenants were the result of negotiation, this one was not. God initiated the covenant as an outward expression of His purpose to never flood the earth again with water and to show mercy to the descendants of Noah.

Noah's Time of Testing

Genesis 7

Noah was six hundred years old when the floodwaters came to the earth. Noah, his sons, his wife, and his sons' wives entered the ark to escape the waters of the flood. Pairs of clean and unclean animals, of birds, and of all creatures that move along the ground, male and female, came to Noah and entered the ark, as God had commanded Noah. After seven days, floodwaters came into the earth.

When the catastrophe came, the waters that were unleashed were twofold; the breaking up of the "fountains of the deep" from the ground and the opening of the windows of the firmament. The tears from heaven tormented the earth for forty days and forty nights. Inside that ship must have been a time of deep turmoil and testing that no one could understand but God. Their future was the only hope they had to withstand the hour.

As the waters began to recede, Noah and his family prepared for a new day. God gave Noah the covenant of the rainbow as an assurance. He even entrusted him with the authority over the animal kingdom to do as he willed. The sight of the earth after the flood must have been terrifying. The sense of loss and the carnage surely made it a solemn task to begin to recover the earth. Nothing could have prepared Noah and his family for the horror of that day.

Noah lived an extremely long life with great hardship and solemn responsibility. He literally had the world placed on his shoulders for over a hundred and twenty years. The only thing that must have been harder was watching the hand of God's wrath slowly fall on his unbelieving society. For a week, Noah and his family stayed inside the ark before the flood came. I can only begin to imagine the prayer and the insecurity that must have permeated their souls. Their hearts had to be broken by those who rejected the pleas to repent and trust the warnings that rang out for over a century. Surely, they heard their cries to open the door as the waters swept them away.

The Continuing Sin after the Flood

Genesis 9

When Noah awoke from his wine and found out what his youngest son had done to him, he said, "Cursed be Canaan! The lowest of slaves will he be to his brothers."

The sons of Noah: Shem, Ham and Japheth carried on the same character and reflection of Noah in their family. Yet, when their ancestral flaws began to surface in their lives it began to established the continuing Way of Cain that they were intended to eradicate. Even the most faithful and obedient servant Noah, fell hard and brought the extension of sin into the lives of his sons. Sadly, Ham's attitude was not so forgiving.

The new day for humanity was short lived as Noah fell to drunkenness from the vineyard that he planted. The difficulty of reconstruction and the pressures from the mission had begun to erode the remnant and open the door to the past. The handwriting was on the wall that the deluge was not the complete solution, but only a temporary answer for the sin that covered the planet. A new way had to be found to remove the sting of sin and death. Satan used the gift of God once again to betray his Maker and began again to stoke the fires of dissention. The sense of loss and the anxiety of restarting earth with only seeds, had to weigh heavily on Noah. As Noah fell into drunkenness and seclusion, he left the door opens to an ensuing attack from the tempter to bring a deepening fall into the riddled family of Noah.

The consequence of Noah's sin was compounded in one of his sons. Ham went into Noah's tent and uncovered his father's nakedness. What was this rising disrespect that caused Ham's aggressive rejection of his father? There were two ways that Noah's son could have responded to Noah's shame. He could have covered the sin out of love and respect, but Ham chose to ridicule and expose the sin. Noah's drunkenness and nakedness was certainly shameful, but Ham's response was even more so, as Ham dishonored the Lord and his family. When Noah awakened, and discovered what Ham had done, Ham's heart of sin and rebellion had to be exposed. Not only was it rebellion against his father's authority, but ultimately it was rebellion against God.

Ham's brothers, Shem and Japheth showed respect for their father and forgiveness toward his fall. Rather than make light and trivialize Noah's sin, they treated it with the gravity it deserved. They sought immediately to cover him so that he would be shamed no further. They did not seek to tear down his righteous reputation, but sought to uphold righteousness. They showed not only respect for their father, but also respect for what he stood for as a righteous servant of God. Ham was subject to be the servant of the other two sons of Noah. The rebellious attitude in Ham would one day expose itself further, not only in Ham, but also in Ham's descendants.

Noah's curse was not an empty threat; the descendants of Ham experienced a long history of slavery. This curse was not exclusive to Ham, it plagued the descendants of all three sons. Noah's curse on Canaan did not excuse the wickedness of slavery nor does it mean that Ham's descendants are of less worth in God's eyes than the descendants of the other two brothers. The curse is not to be taken as a comment on the intrinsic value of one group over another. The plague of sin revived in the generations following Noah but the grace of God always returns to shine out in the hearts of men.

The despots of sin began to cry out again in the first wake of human experience after the flood. Even though this was true, God's amazing grace continued to show even through the continuing rebellion of sin and apostasy. The dark night would once again leave an irreverent background for the saving grace of a loving Creator. His patience would again win the night. The Messiah from the prophecy to Eve would eventually come in the True Deliverer, and release mankind from the incarnate evil of this world. It was obvious that it would take a miraculous intervention from our God in the person of His Son to repair the desperate heart of humanity.

The tempter exploited Noah through sin to cause a chain reaction in his family, identical to the assault in Eden. Satan used the descendants of Ham to desecrate God's image with returning the fallen social order from the Way of Cain. With this plan, Satan continued his spell encircling the planet with more intensity. The rain of deception returned to fall upon the earth in a deluge of seduction leading to a new assault. The history of Noah and his sons made it clear that the root of rebellion was not completely extinguished in the flood. The sin from Eden was not to be remedied until the Redeemer would come and sacrifice Himself for the lost.

In the coming days of Babel, the anger of Nimrod reflected that the Way of Cain was only to continue. Tragically, the descendants of Noah began to lead the world again into the culmination of a new order void of God's imprint and his will. The rebellion from the flood would continue its torrent in the following ages, because of the spiritual blindness and the desperate condition seeded in humanity. The Prince of this World's carnival would again strike its assault through the evil soul of a greedy predator.

The Complex Sons of Noah

Genesis 9

The sons of Noah who came out of the ark were Shem, Ham, and Japheth. Ham was the father of Canaan. These were the three sons of Noah, and from them came the people who were scattered over the whole earth.

In the family of Noah, Shem is given priority, Ham comes second, and Japheth is last. The order of Noah's descendants was paramount in the furtherance of mankind after the flood. Man's spiritual needs are always superior, his physical needs are meant to be secondary, and intellectual and philosophical needs are to be last. The Days of Noah had inverted humanity into the image of the Prince of this World.

The waters had parted, but the hope of sin being drowned was still there. This is reflected in all the history of man and the rise and fall of one civilization after another. Ultimately, the demise in history always comes to an end because of spiritual decadence and selfish sin. To Shem is given the mantle of maintaining man's true spirituality; to Ham, was given the task of assuring physical survival and to Japheth was given the art of philosophy. All these attributes of humanity were comprised in these surviving members. Ham was scattered across the earth reaching the furthest parts of the world before his brethren. Ham established the depth of technology and the sophistication that plunged the world once again into an indulgent society.

Japheth followed later in many of these areas and inherited the technology of Ham allowing his society to spend much of their time in creating philosophies that corrupted the minds of men. The reflection of Noah's sons began to spread and bring a renewed culture that would soon spread throughout the region. Each son defined the culture of the area in which they held. Thus, it came about that the pioneering task of re-opening the new world order, rendering it habitable for the spell of the evil one. It was evident that the Great Deluge had not subdued the desperate heart of man as the waters of rebellion would soon rise again.

The spiritual reflection of Noah's sons was based on their pursuits and priorities. The faith in Jehovah God was with Shem's descendants and was kept with them. Contrary, the so-called gods of the early Indo-Europeans of Japheth, were gods of light and celestial worship, but this light was not moral light but rather the illumination of the carnal mind or understanding. The gods of the Hamites were the gods of power, with the absence of a moral code. They were ruthlessness, demanding appropriate sacrifices. The root of eclipsing the root of counterfeiting the true Light now covers the earth from the dissection of humanism.

The deluge did little to spiritually recover the earth. After the cursing of Canaan from Ham and the blessing of Shem and Japheth, we are told that Noah died at 950 years old. This proceeded to the Table of Nations, where we learn the three sons of Noah fathered descendants who became the nations spread out over the earth after the flood.

Spiritual Shem

Genesis 9

May God extend Japheth' territory; may Japheth live in the tents of Shem, and May Canaan be the slave of Japheth."

Shem, the son of Noah was the benefactor of Noah's spiritual destiny. Of the three sons of Noah, Shem knew that the first prophecy given to Eve would be carried through his descendants, and it was up to him and his line to transmit and carry the knowledge of God and the hope of salvation. throughout the generations. The reason he is always listed first could also have to do with the fact that his family line produced the Semitic people, including the Jewish people.

Shem, along with his brothers and their wives, fulfilled God's commandment to begin repopulating the earth. The Book of Genesis tells us that Shem was one hundred years old at the birth of his son, Arpachshad, two years after the deluge. He lived for another five hundred years until his death. Shem's descendants strove to lay the emphasis on the journey for faith and righteousness, the Japheth's descendants put their emphasis on the inquisitive search for understanding and the Hamitic people searched for power.

The dramatic influence that came at the dispersion at Babel was not as drastic to the heirs of Shem, because Shem was the only one of Noah's sons that remained in the area. This area eventually became the cradle of the three major religions: Judaism, Islam, and Christianity. This claimed the lineage that began again after the flood.

Japheth, the Philosopher

Genesis 9

May God extend Japheth's territory; may Japheth live in the tents of Shem, and may Canaan be the slave of Japheth.

Japheth was the youngest son of Noah. He was the father of many tribes inhabiting the east of Europe and the north of Asia. Only Indo-Europeans have continually returned to the fundamental problems of metaphysics: the Aryans in India gave rise to Hindu philosophies, and much later European and New world philosophers. Japheth fathered seven sons: Gomer, Magog, Madai, Javan, Tubal, Meshech, and Tiras. The descendants of Japheth included various maritime peoples as well as the Persians, Greeks, Romans, Scythians, and Macedonians. Japheth's descendants spread out over much of Asia and Europe and, through colonization.

His immediate descendants were smaller than his two brothers. The descendants of Japheth spread all over Europe, more so than any of the other sons of Noah. From this main body of settlers, one group split off and ventured into the East, to Persia and India. To begin with, it is well known that Japheth's name was split into two major divisions and settled in Europe and India. Japheth is usually regarded as the ancestor of the Gog and Magog tribes. The history of Britain can also be traced back to the sons of

Japheth. Historical evidence strongly suggests the first inhabitants of the British Isles were the descendants of Javan, and of Gomer and Magog. The Celts are thought to have created Stonehenge.

Ham, the Inventor

Genesis 10

From these the maritime peoples spread out into their territories by their clans within their nations, each with its own language. The sons of Ham: Cush, Egypt, Put and Canaan.

Ham helped return the earth to the spell of rebellion. Ham's heart of rebellion was exposed when he transgressed against his father. This attitude of resentment in Ham rose not only in Ham, but also in Ham's descendants. Ham became invested in the art of invention and began the line of technology again carried on from the Way of Cain. He started the development of dominant civilization in its more secular aspects. The Indo-Europeans became the cradle of the most inventive people in the world.

According to scripture, Ham migrated southwest into Africa and the surrounding areas of Asia, and became the father of the nations there. The Bible refers to Egypt as "the land of Ham" in several places. The Egyptian word for Egypt was Kemet, meaning "black land." Scholars claim it was in reference to the fertile dark soil along the Nile Valley, not the supposed curse that many speculate that it refers to a curse coloring the skin of Ham. Cush, the son of Ham became the father of the Ethiopians, the Arabians, and the Babylonians. The people of Cush first migrated southward, into Arabia. From Arabia they moved into modern day Ethiopia. The most memorable of Cush's sons was Nimrod, the great hunter and author of the city and Tower of Babel. The first biblical mention of Nimrod is in the Table of Nations. Nimrod founded his kingdom in Babel, where he attempted to build a city and to erect a tower to reach into the stars.

The Rising Table of Nations

Genesis 10

These are the clans of Noah's sons, according to their lines of descent, within their nations. From these the nations spread out over the earth after the flood.

At the outset it is important to examine why Moses provides us with the information of the Table of Nations. Though it is tempting to pass over genealogies, they have much bearing on the original situation Moses addressed was addressing. Genesis Ten does not include an exhaustive list of every single people group on the planet. Because this book was written to the nation of Israel as they were freed from slavery in Egypt, it focuses on those peoples known to the Hebrews. Moreover, though many nations are found in this list, they are not all described in the same detail.

The Table of nations became the extension of the family of Noah. The Table of Nations is a list of the patriarchal founders of seventy nations which descended from Noah through his three sons. The Bible is the source of the accurate history of the nations. Genesis establishes the rising world order, and reveals the characteristics that have determined future history and set the conclusion of each branch of humanity in their journey from the deluge. The revelation of the Table of Nations revealed that Noah had populated the earth to the extent of seventy nations. This revealed that this began the final world order to come. The extension of these nations brought a great deal of the world "the systematized error" that we now live in. Genesis has been found completely accurate from linguistic studies, from archaeology, and from the findings of anthropologists, who have recovered important facts to the lines of migration in ancient times.

Theologically, Genesis implicates the unity of the human race since all nations, are regarded not just through bloodlines, but through spiritual heritage. This implicitly explained Israel's relationship to the nations. Even though God's blessing rested upon Shem's line, the separation of humanity into different peoples and cultures had its purpose of sifting out His purpose. The Lord is the One who allows any society to flourish, and we can look back in history and see how the knowledge and technologies developed even by the pagans. The result of the Table of Nations and the descendants of Noah resumed the plot of the world systematized error through the loins of Ham. The next profound leader, Nimrod, continued the Way of Cain to reestablish the thirst for power and conquest. From Babel was launched a campaign that does not end until the Battle of Armageddon.

Nimrod and the Tower of Babel

Genesis 10

Cush was the father of Nimrod, who became a mighty warrior on the earth. He was a mighty hunter before the Lord; that is why it is said, "Like Nimrod, and a mighty hunter before the Lord." The first centers of his kingdom were Babylon, Uruk, Akkad and Kalneh, in Shinar.

The Prince of Darkness again casts a spell over mankind with another conspiracy to stain planet earth. Nimrod constructed the city and Tower of Babel to revive the Way of Cain. The travesty of no resolution from flooding the earth was apparent as mankind returned to their mad confusion. The process of apostasy would flourish from one empire after another in the dark Way of Cain leading to the ominous Mystery of Lawlessness. Nimrod, another pawn of evil had appeared from the shadow of the Great Deluge.

Nimrod was the grandson of Ham and the great-grandson of Noah. Nimrod started the beginning of the kingdom of Babylon with the city and Tower of Babel. It later reached its zenith under King Nebuchadnezzar of the nation of Babylon. This was the seed of kingdom building that swept the globe under this evil sorcery and began the climb to the final global empire that we now face.

The definition for Nimrod is "the Rebel." This was the perfect name for him. It is a negative definition for a leader of a system that is founded in rebellion against the Creator. Nimrod resumed the rebellion occurring before the flood under the influence of Cain and the fallen ones. Nimrod is exposed as a man thriving for worldly power and he was a mighty hunter. He was without a doubt, a man of great charisma and ability. He also held tremendous influence over the people of Babel as Hitler mesmerized Germany. It was Nimrod's ability as a hunter that his fame was obtained, and ultimately, he rose to a position as the world leader of his time.

Once again, a man with a severe "god" complex chose to rise to the heavens to replace God. The arrogance and deception of the Evil One found another "Jester" to establish his court. Nimrod began the descent of society again turning his power and government into tyranny, and extracting the fear of God into anger in rejection of the Creator. He was so arrogant that he covered the rising tower in pitch, like the ark, in case God went against His Word and flooded the earth again. He was the executor of the Way of Cain after the flood at even a more devilish level.

Babel is composed of two words, "bab" meaning "gate" and "el," meaning "god." It is also derived from the related word in Hebrew, "balal" which means "confusion." The sorcery of "selfism" took root from the original sin of excluding God. This name revealed the pagan idea that "the third eye" or the human mind is the gateway to God. The foundation of Babel, Babylon, and Babylon, the Great are built upon this spiritual deception.

As Nimrod built up cities, both on the Tigris and Euphrates rivers, as his predecessor Cain, he began to instigate religious practices originating before the flood that were directly at odds with the worship of the Lord. Nimrod reestablished the "Mystery Religions" of paganism and self-deification that was handed down through the fallen angels. These twisted beliefs led to the belief that nature and God are in essence the same, and Polytheism, the religious system which establishes multiple gods. These fallen practices were polarized against Monotheism, which is the worship of one God. There is no question that these pagan forms were all rooted in Ancient Babylon.

The final stage of this rebellion was the false deification of Nimrod and his mother. Nimrod was deified as Marduk, the chief god of Babylon. He constructed a religion that included deification and worship of himself as emperor, and the worship of the stars and planets that came from antediluvian astronomy. This was repeated through the pagan nations through the Caesars of the Roman empire. It comes to fruition when the Antichrist claims godhood.

After the deaths of Nimrod and his wife Semiramis, the so-called ancient "Queen of Heaven," this evil royalty, was established by their pagan priests as supreme gods and given the stellar names of Marduk and Astarte. Even Israel was stained by this pagan sickness. Israel and other nations were introduced to the worship of Marduk by the name, Baal which means "lord" or "master."

The Bible reveals that the ultimate source of all this global deception is not anchored in Nimrod or any other man, but rather in the evil character of the one who possesses him, namely Satan. It is amazing that the form of the serpent is found as a thread throughout the scripture and pagan worship and always finds identity in Satan: the serpent of Eden.

Another reflection of this self-worship is the worship of the stars and planets. Babylonian astrology wove its way through history and was based on the realization that the entire universe was created with the earth as the center of the universe. This system of demonic half-truths is known today to Bible scholars as the "Babylonian Mystery Religion." From a biblical point of view this religious system is described as the well-spring for all subsequent false religions.

In time, the true histories of most of the early nations became distorted beyond all recognition. Who would believe, when reading modern commentaries on the Book of Genesis, that so much evidence was available to prove, not its falsity, but its authenticity? It is frightening how vague and isolated the historical and spiritual readings are taking place today. Although scholars have been aware of the existence of the vast body of information through the ages, it is now passed over in silence. The confusion and delusion from the course of this present evil age has deafened the ears of culture from the dark rapids flowing from the days of Noah.

The vein of Babylon is woven throughout history and the Bible. In the Old Testament Babylon went from a city to an all-powerful nation. Babylon gave birth to an empire that ruled the known world and imposed a worldview upon all the peoples that she conquered. She was brutal and anti-God; she was proud and she thought she would reign forever. She then becomes the empire that destroys Jerusalem, burns the temple, and takes the people of God into exile. In the New Testament, the Babylonian Harlot is a falling nation, and a manifesting spirit. She is finalized as the mysterious Harlot that is swallowed up by the Antichrist through fire; but in the end, like Jezebel, she is judged, despoiled, and cast down.

There is a grave mystery lying silently in the shifting sands of the original Babylon? The evil one has plotted through history to bring fame and fortune from this forsaken land by inflicting exile and turmoil upon the people of God. This coming to fruition at this moment of time as the planet is impacted by the trauma in the Middle East. In the Book of Revelation, the Mysterious Harlot of Babylon is revealed as a wicked global city-state with an abominable religious system. She join with the Antichrist and the Beast for the final generation replicating the days of Noah. This evil political, religious, and economical global order will sweep across the world involving ten entities with the Antichrist corrupting everything it touches. This Beast is ridden by this Harlot pouring her cup out causing the kings and the nations to be drunk on the wine of her fornication.

The Dispersion at the Tower of Babel

Genesis 11

But the Lord came down to see the city and the tower the people were building. The Lord said, "If as one people speaking the same language, they have begun to do this, then nothing they plan to do will be impossible for them. Come, let us go down and confuse their language so they will not understand each other." So, the Lord scattered them from there over all the earth, and they stopped building the city. That is why it was called Babel because there the Lord confused the language of the whole world. From there the Lord scattered them over the face of the whole earth.

The Way of Cain resurfaced, starting the Babylonian "mystery world order" would end under the foolish son of Nebuchadnezzar as the hand of God writes their doom on their banquet hall and within hours fell captive to the next empire of the Persians. God will be patient but He will not be mocked. Whether it is the raging nations that thrive for supremacy or his own nation of people that backslide into unbelief, men will reap what they sow if they do not fall into the arms of their Redeemer in these days of desperation. The planet had once again found its way through the sin again become unified under the same evil spell.

Since the Tower of Babel, the tyrants that have tried to unite the world under domination have failed miserably, because God over and over confounds the communication that would try to bring unity the the cohesion between cultures that has never won the day. From Nimrod to Nebuchadnezzar, from the Caesars to Hitler: they all failed to reach their zenith because God would not allow it. Even the Antichrist will be destroyed at the Messiah's triumph in the Valley of Decision.

❧ Chapter Five ❧

The Horrendous Way of Cain

1 John 3

Do not be like Cain, who belonged to the evil one and murdered his brother. And why did he murder him? Because his own actions were evil and his brothers were righteous.

The Way of Cain was one of the most understated mysteries in the Bible. Almost everyone knows that Cain murdered his brother Abel, but very little is understood concerning his impact in the Days of Noah. The two greatest reasons that the Lord provoked the Great Flood are both great mysteries. The first was the mysterious Way of Cain mentioned in finality in the Book of Jude. The second was the fallen angels leaving their first estate, and then crossing an unspeakable boundary with sexual relations with women and angels.

After Cain refused to repent for murdering his brother Abel, he was banished from the presence of the Lord and started his own path of unbelief, trusting in himself. It seeded the eventual development of the first great rebellion, defying God and restarting the evil campaign that would eventually conquer the heart of man. In conspiracy with the Prince of Darkness, Cain pioneered the first world order. This first great rebellion would even find its way past the deluge into the brave new world of the city and Tower of Babel.

We have now discovered through the ages that the enemy always finds a lawless rebel to help invoke his systematized error to harness his narcissistic will on the masses. This was Satan's first lawless pawn with even murder on his resume. Far past the sin from the garden, Cain had attained the attributes of his new found father, the author of confusion. Most have no understanding who and what had inspired Cain to murder his brother, defy his Maker and pioneer a new insipid culture that would provoke his Lord to flood the creation and detour God's plan for the history of mankind.

The Way of Cain pioneered the coming world order through the ages, and the extending sphere of influence that gave the Prince of this World the inroad he was looking for. The collusion with the fallen angels and the Way of Cain cut the way to conspire against the gates of heaven. The word for way, "hodos" in the Greek means "a road." It indicates a direction, a way of life, and a belief system with or without relationship with God. It is defined by Jesus as "the broad road that leads to destruction, or the narrow way that leads to life." The narrow way was tread by Abel beginning the refusal to embrace sin and plea for the need for redemption.

At the end of the New Testament, Jude speaks out against ungodly men "who pervert the grace of our God into a license for immorality and deny the authority of Jesus Christ, having taken the Way of Cain, rejecting God's will." The Way of Cain was based on following your own desires and embracing their own moral authority. It was the rejection and betrayal of heaven and was the depth and foundation in evil.

The first family's expulsion from Eden was soon followed by the coming birth of a firstborn as a major event. Eve was expecting that her first son would be the "seed of the woman" referred to in the promise of redemption from God that would bruise the serpent's head for redemption. She perceived that her first son would deliver the family back into God's favor and purpose. This was not a broken promise but an impatient misunderstanding.

Then Eve had her second son, Abel. Little did Eve understand that these two sons were to part the waters between salvation and judgment. The two sons differed radically in their moral character and devotion. Cain was energetic, ambitious, resourceful, and a man to make his own mark in the world. This conflict was that he was also a man of bad temper, selfish, cruel, hard, and resentful of his brother. Abel was quiet, affectionate, and patient. Cain could not have been more polarized from his brother. This set the stage for the horror of the next fall of humanity, that was brought to the surface soon after leaving Eden with the darkest point in man's short history.

Am I My Brother's Keeper?

Genesis 4

Then the LORD said to Cain, "Where is your brother Abel?"

"I don't know," he replied. "Am I my brother's keeper?"

"Am I my brother's keeper?" was the anthem that exposed the fallen heart of Cain that was filled with pride and arrogance toward God and his brother. This quote from Cain totally exhibited his hardened heart and his fearless and careless attitude toward his Creator. Cain's heart was never right with God and his refusal to repent of his sin crouching at his door finally conquered him.

As sin always does without repentance, it plummeted to the ultimate depth. His dormant personal relationship with God had made his human relationships toxic because they became self-centered and were based on his own desires with no commitment. Cain sat on the throne of his own life and he was determined that not even God would change that. No matter how great your gift may be, if your heart is wrong, then it will produce nothing.

After sin entered this new world because of Adam and Eve's disobedience, God established a sacrificial system and explained that without the shedding of blood there is no forgiveness for sin. Abel faithfully brought a young lamb as a sacrifice for his sins, but Cain thought it was unnecessary to obey God's commandment so precisely. So, he brought an offering of his own works, some produce from the field. Cain watched with jealous anger as fire came down from heaven and consumed Abel's sacrifice, but left his own offering untouched. The Lord lovingly urged Cain to humble himself and obey, but Cain stubbornly persisted in his rebellion. Abel also tried to gently reason with his older brother, but Cain flew into a rage. By the time he regained his senses, Abel's bloody body lay still at his feet, changing the axis of love to hatred.

Although Cain was brilliant and gifted, he bowed to his lower base and shook the earth. As his parents revealed when they were naked and they felt no shame, Cain extended sin as he felt no shame for rejecting God's will, ultimately murdering his own brother. As Lucifer, he deferred to believe that he was the reason for his own brightness and he refused God's glory and counsel. He was arrogant and unteachable. The hope for his repentance from sin faded even more as he grew in stature and accomplishment. It instantly made him the coming target for the evil one's further seduction.

Many believe that stupidity and ignorance are one and the same, yet nothing is further from the truth. Some of the brightest people I have met are the most ignorant. Ignorance is from the root, "to ignore." It is to refuse the truth and to dwell in selfish perception. Cain's pride and anger that led him to murder his own brother was sparked by his jealousy and conceit. Cain wanted things his way and took it out on the brother who humbly obeyed his Lord and Master.

Hardness of heart makes it impossible to hear from God and it binds you up in sin and self-esteem. Cain refused accountability to Cain's hardened heart caused his concern about his punishment was far more important than his brother's blood crying from the ground. God then pronounced a curse upon Cain, and when Cain complained about his sentence, the Lord placed a mark upon him lest future generations take revenge for this first homicide.

After murdering his loving brother, how could Cain have mocked God and the brother he just massacred with the statement, "Am I my brother's keeper?" How could a young man raised in the presence of God feel nothing about lying to God and have no conscience about murdering his brother? The heart of Cain loved one thing, Cain. How had Cain inherited the heart of Lucifer and the devilish serpent from his former estate? Cain from the beginning was a self-worshipper. The Lord grieved in his heart that Cain led mankind into following in his wicked footsteps as Lucifer had led his insolent angels away from their loving God. It was not in him to esteem others higher than himself, because of the sense of entitlement. Selfish evil was not just restricted to Cain. It was then cultivated in the culture around him that he inherited through his sin, birthing "selfism" that has now riddled the globe.

The Curse Upon Cain

Genesis 4

The Lord said, "What have you done? Listen! Your brother's blood cries out to me from the ground. Now you are under a curse and driven from the ground, which opened its mouth to receive your brother's blood from your hand. When You will be a restless wanderer on the earth."

The word for sin in the Greek is "Horatio," meaning "missing the mark." Cain was a master from the beginning at missing the mark faith and truth, being buried in selfism. When we sin, we often do so with the futile hope that we shall receive the maximum amount of pleasure with the minimum penalty. This was the twisted perception that Cain leaned upon. The foundational sin of Cain helps us to understand the toxicity of Cain's character and his defective heart that brought the fruit of decadence and terrible retribution. Sin chased Cain through his life entire life because of his refusal to confess and repent.

The ground had been cursed on the account of Adam and now the earth had been stained with the innocent blood of Abel as it cried out to God for justice. The time for repentance had passed and now came the sentence. He had left the Lord no choice but to isolate him and discipline Cain to learn the folly of his ways. God chose to focus upon depriving Cain of his only skill, which was to work as a tiller of the ground, hoping he would repent from his heart. The previous flawed offering from the ground is what had instigated Abel's murder. It was a bloodless sacrifice that had no regard for sin or forgiveness. This continued the cycle of Cain's arrogant attitude that was centered to try to humble Cain from his defective ways.

God's second judgment upon Cain stated that he would be a fugitive, and a wanderer upon the earth. We find that Cain is banished from the presence of God and that he became a restless wanderer never to return to a home with God and family. This bitter judgment matched the curse of Lucifer being cast from the heavens and the throne of God. It is obvious that Cain continued and followed the bitter road of Satan. Down the road, Cain was met on his path by the fallen angels that would ease his loneliness and concern over the cursed ground and educate him in the ways of lawlessness. Cain sadly became a vessel of destruction because of his arrogance and his refusal to walk the path of mercy and hope.

The Fatal Broad Way of Cain

1 John 3

Do not be like Cain, who belonged to the evil one and murdered his brother. And why did he murder him? Because his own actions were evil and his brother's were righteous.

After Cain's banishment not only had he aligned himself with the Prince of this World, but he also employed the "secret knowledge of the hidden arts from the fallen ones." This seeded the first civilization through Cain's creation of cities, weapons and an entire system that was alienated from the Creator. Cain then found his way to a place called "Nod." The word "Nod" meant "wandering" which described the rebel Cain's destiny as he was cast out of the protective area of paradise, he became the first tyrannical leader. He lived in the place called Nod and became a nomad separated from God and his heritage. Sadly, he led his influenced clan into total darkness and into the full rebellion against the Lord.

Cain began his way to replace the way of God and his responsibility to account for his own way. Satanic inspiration became the author of mechanical inventions with grand schemes and devices that distanced him from any dependence upon God. He led his clan to a system of selfishness and sensuality. When Cain lost the power of the soil that was made unfruitful by his brother's drenching blood; it forced him to find the different way which the Prince of this World gladly accommodated. He led a life of vanity with his soul utterly void of eternal purpose; in search of his own way.

Cain joined with his angelic renegades by deluging the earth with self-based religion and control through idolatry. It began the humanism that is embracing us today, a godhood without Christ, or remission through blood, or pardon from man's sinful condition. Through the twisted relationship with the angelic rebels, Cain was founded upon lawless "selfism" with a thirst for power and control. As Cain was expunged from society, he went even deeper into exile., creating the first "world order."

By Cain's hand, Mesopotamia became the cradle of technology and civilization. The Fertile Crescent and the Tigris and Euphrates rivers gave birth to the line of Cain to the first "Great Society." Tragically, Cain's followers chose to create the first secular tribe. It is so important in whom we follow. Men then began to worship the creation over the Creator. The worship of the sun, the moon and the stars replaced the worship of God. Man became the center of his own desires and things fell so far that even cannibalism and human sacrifice surfaced. Rebellion against God became the way of life and the Way of Cain emerged in the most graphic ways possible.

How tragic that Cain took his mother's mantle of ruling his own life at the expense of her relationship with God. The Way of Cain then grew tentacles with the hidden support of the angelic renegades creating the new civilization. Cain and his family then developed musical instruments and other entertainment inspired through the spiritual deception to break the monotony of having lost their real life in relationship with God.

The mystery of alchemy was then introduced by "the fallen ones" that spanned from establishing tools and weapons from metal, to build and protecting the cultic cities that Cain created. The ancients found how secret ways to perfect matter through natural process. This is where they claimed the God of nature came from, and all the present religions. But it was always "secret." To speak of it was to die. The claim of alchemy says it has its base in everything from astrology, religion, the Secret Societies, and many sorceries established at this time.

The origin of Gnosticism which still pollutes the earth was birthed with its godless philosophy. The invention of government and pagan religion was directed by the Way of Cain and brought the seeds that would develop the empirical dominance that began again at Babel and is the source of our systematized error of today. This began mankind walking in full step with Satan and his rebels. When man doesn't have the true Lord, he has always deferred to systematized government and self-based religion.

The angelic pagan religion that Cain produced covered himself in the veneer of worshiping the Creator but it was anything but that. Still professing God but beneath it was the selfish desire to take God's authority and sit on his throne in repeat of Satan's assault. He began the practice of using manmade "idols" in human worship. The first such idols were figures of a man and female deity, no doubt representing Cain and his wife, with whom he built his first city. False religion and fallen culture came to the forefront.

The first kings of the earth were called "priest-kings," and Cain became the High Priest of his own religious system that is still mocking the Lord even today. Cain was the originator of the coming Babylonian mystery religion that is in the loins of our present apostasy. He established his own form of religious empire, with sensual, earthy services, compelling tithes to be paid by his worshippers, creating lavish "temples" with male and female prostitution, the origins of the worship of Canaanite abominations which God condemned in the time of Moses. We are now seeing this idolatry come to fruition in another bloodless form.

The impact of Cain's arrogant ways set himself against everything and everyone that had been valuable to him, especially God. When they provoked Jesus into answering what commandment was the most important, Jesus responded, "Love the Lord your God with all your heart and with all your soul and with your entire mind and love your neighbor as yourself." The response of repentance would have spared Cain's soul.

The Foundational Wicked Spiritual Deception

Psalm 78

They would not be like their ancestors—
a stubborn and rebellious generation,
whose hearts were not loyal to God,
whose spirits were not faithful to him.

The essence of rebellion bled from Lucifer at the throne in heaven before man's creation to the Garden of Eden unto the heart of Cain. Lucifer was a conceale rebel in his heart and he had lost his fear or reverence for God. Cain followed and was the first religious man that demanded to reach godhood in his own way and on his own terms. But as you cannot tell the earth to stop spinning, man cannot stop spinning the web of his own way.

Cain became a powerful leader and he framed his entire clan into following his deceitful and controlling ways. Cain created a radical new path where one person could control others into a cultic order to prosper for themselves. Cain's descendants created a system of slavery that would eventually engulf the entire planet. It was a system that first provided necessities and then gradually shifted to luxury and pleasure. Cain's inheritance from the fallen angels was subtle, and secretive, sharing his new religious knowledge, and divine secrets, and protecting them from the so-called unwarranted dominance of their Creator.

Cain devised man-made religion based on works, indulgence versus sacrifice, and the worship of false gods, the original "Baals," with himself the chief "god" since he was the progenitor of his race, and considered himself the "Messiah to come," as the prefigure of the Antichrist. He followed the Prince of Darkness through every step. He employed earthly goddesses and gods, which are found by many archaeologists throughout Africa, the Middle East, Europe, and Asia. His system of paganism was massive and seductive. Incredibly, they are even found on our continent since the Days of Noah which has a fantastic answer that we will uncover later.

The fingerprints of the Way of Cain are apparent in every corner of our world today. This self-centered system of error has polluted the entire globe. The New Global Order is seething with the unified deception from the Days of Noah. The all-seeing eye on our dollar bill and capital reflects the unity under our own godhood. The world has also gone wild with the fascination of aliens and their abductions in their imprints. I remember when "Chariots of the Gods" came out and the explosion of interest covered our nation. Today, there are volumes of shows focused on extra-terrestrials that mask the former activity of the fallen watchers that infected society from the beginning.

In the angelic tradition, there were a special elite order of angelic beings created by God to be earthly shepherds of the first primal humans. It was their task to observe and watch over the emerging human species and report back on their progress. Their intervention was tightly monitored and meant to intervene only when necessary. However, they were confined by the divine prime directive not to interfere in human will. One of the angelic responsibilities were to guard and protect the residents of the earth even on a personal basis.

Even today, we are warned to be careful because we may be entertaining angels unaware. So many have crossed the path of these angelic beings at many times without a clue of their presence. They often clothe themselves in human form but they were never to embrace human form in illicit intervention or to become violators instead of protectors. Unfortunately, Satan and his "fallen Watchers" subvert God's order often in silent assault of the unaware. They invade humanity and become their seducers with tragic repercussions for both themselves and society.

The Dark Line of Cain

Genesis 4

Cain made love to his wife, and she became pregnant and gave birth to Enoch. Cain was then building a city, and he named it after his son Enoch. To Enoch was born Irad, and Irad was the father of Mehujael, and Mehujael was the father of Methushael, and Methushael was the father of Lamech.

With unconditional love and the pure mercy of grace, the first murderer comes face to face not with death but with a second chance. Although Cain's life would never be the same, the Lord allowed him to live and to try to learn from his mistakes. Cain did not go unpunished but correction and discipline followed him the rest of his life.

The story of Cain's life unfortunately becomes the story of a man with no remorse, bitterness, and blind arrogance. He exalted himself in defiance of God's commandments, and used his gifting from God to build a world system to glorify himself and to defeat God's plan. His anger and pride led him and his descendants to align with the satanic plot to repeat the history of the fallen angels. With their alliance and Cain's sinful nature, cities flourished with a sensual foundation.

Cain's line attracted many fallen converts while Seth's line dwindled to a small remnant. The promise of power and selfish pleasure began to seduce and leaven his entire culture. Cain knew only too well that the stain from his brother's blood would be visited upon him until the seventh generation, but he ignored any retribution from God. He endeavored, to immortalize his name by governing as he became the architect and builder of a new way that was not new at all.

Cain named his first city Enoch, and he founded six other cities. He introduced a change in the ways of simplicity wherein men had lived before God, and he authored a system of "selfism" which became the heart of the Way of Cain. He corrupted the innocent and while they knew nothing of his true motives, he changed the world into cunning craftiness with the assistance of the Prince of Darkness.

The Sifting of the Line of Cain

Jude 1

Woe to them! For they have gone in the way of Cain. These are spots in your feasts of charity, when they feast with you, feeding them without fear: clouds without water, carried about of winds, trees whose fruit withered, without fruit, twice dead, plucked up by the roots;

The murder of Abel split the family of God, some chose the light and some chose the darkness and fractured mankind into spiritual divorce. From the first family of Adam, the sifting between the faithful and faithless began to take place. The vein of evil that began with the birth of sin from Adam and Eve had taken root immediately. Within one generation, murder had found its way into the family of Adam through Cain's apostate attitude and his selfish will. Cain murdered his brother out of a jealous rage because he was accepted for being obedient and following God's will. Cain refused God's grace and forgiveness and was banished from the family of God. He actually felt that he was the victim. The art of blaming God and others permeates our culture from the Way of Cain.

There were still two apparent branches to the family of Adam. They were the line of Cain, and the new line of Seth. Seth then followed the line of faith that would lead to Noah and his sons. Cain continued the satanic line of rebellion that would be drowned in the approaching storm. These two opposing lines came to fruition and were separated by the flood. The difference between the faithful line of Seth and the rebellious line of Cain was as graphic as light and darkness. In Seth's line the seventh man from Adam was Enoch, a type of the Church who was "raptured" as he walked with God. Enoch is a profound character and writer from the Days of Noah.

In the line of Cain, the seventh extension from Adam was Lamech. He led his tribe in Cain's worldly ways. The fruit didn't fall far from the tree. He was a confessed murderer and the first polygamist. Cain's children introduced the earth to godless civilization based on the exaltation of man, who by their own achievements would try to redeem themselves. From these children came ranching, manufacturing, the arts, music, and entertainment.

The names of Cain's children spoke a lot about his identity and his perpetual anger. Enoch, the city was a debacle. Cain's reputation was enough to keep everyone away. Irad, was the third generation and Cain's seed still had a very difficult life. Irad ironically meant "fugitive." Cain's children remained out of relationship with God and out of touch with other people because of the root of bitterness. "And Irad became the father of Mehujael." Mehujael means "smitten of God." Cain's resentment continued to the fourth generation. They were still known as the rejected ones living under God's curse and punishment, but they no longer had to wander like fugitives. In the Way of Abel came Lamech who had three sons; Jabal a livestock breeder, Jubal a musician, Tubal-Cain a toolmaker, and a daughter Naamah. From these children came farming, manufacturing, arts and music, and entertainment. In just seven generations we see a surfacing civilization; cities in which to live, leisure and entertainment, and industry.

Toward the end of the family of Cain, murder was revisited by Cain's descendant Lamech. He sings a mysterious song that alludes back to Cain's curse. He sings of murdering two people who he fought and claims that if Cain was avenged seven-fold than Lamech should be avenged seventy-sevenfold. Many theologians label this scripture as the "Song of the Sword," and it tells of Lamech's boasting of killing two men with the first use of the sword after its creation by his son, the first blacksmith, Tubal-Cain.

With the help of Cain's civilization, and the creation of weaponry, Lamech shouts that he will avenge himself seventy times sevenfold, without the help of God. This proclamation spoke just how far evil had spread in the inverted moralism in the Way of Cain. The leaven of Cain's sin had swallowed up the broad inhabitants of the earth in the continuing assault of Satan upon the remnant of God. Sadly, the earth was ripened for destruction. It is tragic that the deluge of this entire line of carnality surfaced quickly in the descendants of Noah. Although sin was present in both lines, there could not have been a more polarized way of life.

The Mark on Cain

Genesis 4

But the Lord said to him, "Not so; anyone who kills Cain will suffer vengeance seven times over." Then, the Lord put a mark on Cain so that no one who found him would kill him.

The Mark of Cain was one of the other mysteries related to Cain that many have wondered about for centuries. In the Hebrew, the word does not identify the exact nature of the mark that God bestowed upon Cain. Some propose that the mark was a scar, or a tattoo. The mark of Cain was truly a sign of God's protection; the mark itself was not the curse. God punished Cain by sending him away from his family, from all he knew, and that he could no longer find fulfillment in farming the way he had his entire life. His people created the cities because the earth would not yield fruit to him anymore. Whatever the case, the precise nature of the mark was not the actual focus. Nothing was more branded than the desperate heart of Cain. It tragically testified of who now owned him, not the deception that it was himself. It really branded him above all with the mark as the first murderer. This mark identified Cain, and set him apart in exclusion.

Jewish and Christian scholars have proposed a variety of explanations to describe this mark. The Bible not only connects the mark with divine protection, but it links the tattoo that God placed upon Cain, imaging it as a badge of shame. This mark was an actual letter from the original alphabet. It was ironically used in the story of the "Scarlet Letter" that was an "A" to represent the sin of adultery. There is a saying used that someone is a "marked man." This is defined as a curse on someone who is not liked or trusted or who is in danger of being harmed for their ways. This was the case with Cain.

Cain's mark has always been attached with the coming Mark of the Beast. The peril of narcissism has deluged the planet today at an unprecedented rate and is a signal of the forecast of the coming mark of doom. The most pervasive traits are lack of empathy, a sense of grandiosity, and seeking excessive admiration of self. All of these were apparent in Cain's relationships, even with God. The mantra of "it's all about me" was the cancer spread by Cain's heart and attitude that no one can tell me what to do. The warped idea that we can come to God on our own terms is fatal in not being able to align with the truth; not expecting the truth to align with us.

The mark of Cain was God's promise to offer Cain divine protection from premature death with the stated purpose of preventing anyone from killing him. This has bled into the heresy of relativism that has given to the way that "all roads lead to God." This has now become a pandemic and a bloodless global coup rejecting any accountability or reverence to the One who made us in his image. This led to the worship of the image of the Beast that will soon falsely resurrect in a new rebuilt temple in Jerusalem.

Returning to the Way of Cain

Jude 1

Yet these people slander whatever they do not understand, and the very things they do understand by instinct as irrational animals do will destroy them. Woe to them! They have taken the way of Cain.

Ironically, Burger King, the fast-food chain tapped in years ago to the mantra for this generation with the slogan, "Have it your way!" Now, they have an added mantra of "You rule!" Sadly, this is the genius of our age, yet it is a cancer of the soul that has contaminated us from the very beginning. The two prevalent perceptions of the day are God is "mythic" with no relevance, or He is whatever we perceive Him to be. Cain refused God and His authority because he thought he knew better. One of the deadliest beliefs is that God restricts us or wants His way for Himself, not because we are His children and He wants to guide us to protect us. The Apostle Paul told the Corinthians that "he feared that that would be seduced as Eve away from the simple and pure devotion."

The Way of Cain has such a far greater impact even today than we can ever imagine. When sin crouched at the door of Cain from his anger towards God and his brother, Abel, his sin not only became his master, but so did Satan, yet he thought he was his own man. He sojourned out of his father's house right into the arms of the Father of Lies and his fallen angels. His course was set with the dangerous chemistry of non-repentance, rebellion, and arrogance. His separation from God was replaced with a slithering alliance with the fallen regime that drooled for a brilliant rebel like Cain. Their blueprint and their forbidden knowledge inspired him for revenge against God. As we now face the return of Christ and the present evil apostate generation separated from God, we will see a king, the Antichrist as a mockery of Cain.

The Book of Jude is a prescription for us living in the last days concerning the dreadful Way of Cain. It exposes in full detail the heart of what we are facing in this great apostasy and the symptoms that we have inherited from the Days of Noah. When God is removed from the center of life, the gates of hell are opened, leaving no protection from our angelic predators. The Lord had to remove His hand from Noah's generation as Cain's seed was completely deceived by the godlessness and "selfism. The Spirit of God continued to dwell with a remnant such as Noah and Enoch, as He warned them of the impending judgment by water. They understood the future baptism of the planet was inevitable. There was no lack of light; the tragedy was the darkness in the hearts of the inverted culture.

The convicting truth was that humanity had divorced them from the Lord and the wretchedness of man became profound and dominant, but God knew that every imagination, or purpose, of the thoughts of man's heart, would be only evil continually. This was the cistern of depravity of self-serving that seeded this dark and perverted generation and drove them into giving their domain over to the seduction of the army of apostate angels lurking in the shadows. Cain was married the way of evil, the way of spiritual ruin and disaster. Cain became the first of many who would be called the "son of perdition," "son of hell," and "son of doom. He had more to do with the extension from the fall of man after murdering his brother than any person in history excluding Judas Iscariot.

Sadly, even after the cleansing of the earth by the deluge, the rebellion escalated after the flood at the city and Tower of Babel. The corrupt world system eventually found new roots through Nimrod and his followers in the city and Tower of Babel. Our own nation morphed from the Industrial Revolution as we fled into cities from the farms thirsting after wealth and pleasure. Along with came the moral decay and lawlessness that fermented in the Roaring Twenties. The erosion of government, education, and materialism slowly became godless even more after the turbulent Sixties.

❦ Chapter Six ❧

The Invasion of the Watchers

The Original Glorious Angels

Job 38

"Where were you when I laid the earth's foundation? Tell me, if you understand. Who marked off its dimensions? Surely you know! Who stretched a measuring line across it? On what were its footings set, or who laid its cornerstone, while the morning stars sang together and all the angels shouted for joy?

There are many who understand that angels are the members of a previous superior creation of spiritual beings, who were created before the world ever began. There are many myths and many truths that people believe about them. The fact that God had created a realm of personal beings before mankind should help broaden our understanding of God's creation, of what He was previously doing, and how He has worked through eternity. It also explains the history of conflict that is now raging on our globe. It is what we don't see that is so dangerous, and it has helped trap humanity in carnal pursuit in the heart of sensuality.

There are many types of angels with many functions described in the Bible. Angels are God's original creatures created eons ago to carry out the worship and administration of God's order in the third heavens. They were created in beauty and wisdom to help the Lord carry out his will. In the beginning, their relationship with the Creator was dazzling adoration and respect. The faithful angels are spoken of as "the holy ones." They surround the Lord and His throne like a beautiful garment. The relationship with God and the angels was deeply passionate and fulfilling until the unthinkable rebellion led by Lucifer swept a third of the angels into rebellion with him.

The study of angels or the doctrine of angelology is one of the ten major categories of theology. As we search through the Scriptures, we find that there are numbers of different ranks of angels: cherubim, seraphim, and others. They all have specific job descriptions from the military commander of the Lord's hosts to the principal announcers of events involving the Messiah. Angels can materialize, take people by the hand, eat meals with mankind, and even indulge in combat. They often appear in the form of men. Hebrews tells us that many have even entertained angels unaware. I have had some extensive examples of angelic experiences myself.

We must understand our place as a creation and that man is not the highest form of created being, although our estate changes at the eternal threshold and we will even judge angels. It is sad today how spiritual neglect has been replaced with fascination even with the carnal perception of angels. Yet this topic through gullible interest has driven many into the arms of the occult and dark messengers of evil, that masquerade as angels of light, like Lucifer. They are also confused by the myth of extraterrestrials that are in truth fallen angels.

We will delve into the controversial matter that involves the assaulting rebellious angels that conspired with Lucifer after the fall of Adam and Eve. There are grave mysteries that drove our planet into its darkest hour. The encounter with the fallen angels termed, "Watchers" warped the purpose of God and brought the horrendous deluge upon our planet. This chapter will deal with the angelic presence that crusaded in Genesis Six in the days of Noah. The entire course of human history radically changed in the dark falling age of these evil predators. They were a great cause in God's anguishing decision to flood the earth. These repeating horrific influences now are haunting the globe with even more fervor.

Their Home in the Third Heavens

2 Corinthians 2

A man in Christ who fourteen years ago was caught up to the third heaven. Whether it was in the body or out of the body I do not know, God knows. And I know that this man, whether in the body or apart from the body I do not know, but God knows, was caught up to paradise and heard inexpressible things, things that no one is permitted to tell.

Many Christians do not understand that the abode of the   heavens is divided into three separate entities. The Bible speaks of each of these realms clearly. The atmospheric realm or the first heavens are comprised of the air that we breathe as well as the space that immediately surrounds the earth. The technical term for this is the troposphere. It extends about twenty miles above the earth. The space above this is called the stratosphere. The connection of the first and second heavens brings a ferocious amount of heat when space craft enter the first heavens when we travel in space.

The second heavens are expansive and cover a dimension that we peer into with our new technology. The celestial heavens refer to outer space as the stellar heavens. It includes the universe, the galaxies, the sun, the moon, and the stars. The stars are seemingly endless and the distance between all of them is staggering but they end as a canopy at the final heavens. It is recorded that it would take ten thousand years at the speed of light to get to the next star. It took our recent satellite four hours at the speed of light to get the signal here from Pluto. There is no possible way to comprehend the edge of the universe from our atmosphere, at least not yet.

The Bible is clear that our God is not restricted to anyone of these tangible places. In fact, He is omnipresent which means He can occupy as many places at any time that He desires but his home is hidden in the spiritual third heavens. I will not begin to attempt to describe this realm of indescribable beauty. I have never been to God's home but I am sure it is magnificent. The Apostle Paul had an immeasurable experience when he was translated to the paradise of God in the third heavens. He said that he saw things so incredible that it was unlawful to speak of them. The third heavens are God's dwelling place with His remaining faithful angels. This is the cradle of eternity and God's throne until the release of the new heaven and new earth after the return of Christ.

All the angels dwelt in this arena until the first angelic rebellion. When Lucifer and his renegades were expelled from the third heavens for their betrayal, they were cast down to the second heavens as sojourners with no home. They were wanderers like Cain as he lost his place with God. This identification is probably why they chose Cain as the pioneer of rebellion on the globe. These renegades warned about interfering in the first heavens and with man's new domain when it was created. It will be in eternity before we can understand the magnitude of the impact of this fall. They had wandered the stars aimlessly until they targeted God's new interest with the planet earth.

God's former archangel returned to pollute the Lord's new creation with his same devices. Lucifer's two greatest sins that occurred in the third heavens surfaced once again. The very first was pride and then came his betrayal. The sin of pride was the heart of original sin. It was this sin, we're told, which transformed Lucifer, an anointed cherub of God, the very "seal of perfection, full of wisdom and perfect in beauty," into Satan, the devil, the father of lies, the one for whom hell itself was created. Lucifer, the morning star imploded like a black hole placing a dagger in the heart of our eternal beloved Creator again. He learned nothing but rage from his original sin. The stain of sin covered Satan like a dark robe and God's new creation spun out of control through his sinister motives. He began to orchestrate a more deviant rebellion than the one he conspired in the third heavens. Sins and lies are the only thing Satan can take credit for in his miserable existence.

As Satan veiled in the serpent came to earth, the birthing of sin began a chain reaction that we are living in its climax in this final hour. We have to redeem the time, because the days are evil. Time is a gift from God, and none of us know how much of it we are allotted. Only God knows how much time each of us has on this earth to make decisions that will impact eternity.

The Paradigm Shift to Humanity

Genesis 3

Then the man and his wife heard the sound of the Lord God as he was walking in the garden in the cool of the day, and they hid from the Lord God among the trees of the garden. But the Lord God called to the man, "Where are you?"

This same question is ringing today in the hearts of the remnant as we witness our reeling prodigal planet engulfe by the same "Great Lie" the we are gods with no accountability. As Adam, the mass of humanity has no idea what their calling is. They know where they live, they no where they work, but what is their calling? Tragically how many even care?

To Noah's generation, the Lord warned He will not always strive with men as He brought retribution with the deluge. But He first called Noah out of his perverted age to work out his salvation by the works of his hands. He set in stone the appeal by Soloman for today that "God has set eternity in the heart of man. Noah's reverence and vision began a remnant that is pursuing God's eternal will today. Even today's nominal church has little understanding of our eternal mandate to serve God as we they demand Him for service. We are all not witnessing the global flood of "self service" as we reap the whirlwind.

As we face the rapture of the faithful remnant, we were given a pattern in the godly man named Enoch that rejected the course of the present evil age for His eternal relationship with His Lord. His single hearted devotion was his entry into paradise before his time. He gave us the perfected example of who God is looking for today to sweep from the glode before the gates of the Tribulation open.

The Witness of Faithful Enoch

Hebrews 11

By faith Enoch was taken from this life, so that he did not experience death: "He could not be found, because God had taken him away." For before he was taken, he was commended as one who pleased God.

Except for Noah, Enoch was the most prolific man of God in the line of Seth. He was a great teacher, writer, and a prophet. Enoch was also the only person ever to be raptured in the Old Testament with the exclusion of the experiences of Moses and Elijah. He was defined as walking with God until the day he was raptured. His whole being was wrapped up in loving God, warning the lost and spreading God's love to others in teaching and writing. He was a first fruit of what the church should be committed to today. It is tragic that some of our Christian forefathers rejected his writings as inspired and excluded them from the cannon of scriptures. It is even a reason for part of the blindness in the times we are living.

Enoch was responsible for many books that are not in the Bible but the Book of Enoch was originally accepted by our Jewish forefathers. It is considered a great holy writing that speaks intensely on spiritual warfare, fallen angels, and the realm of battle in the days that he lived. It is the most expounding writing on the dark days of Noah. The Book of Enoch is a great Jewish work of antiquity. There are even references where Christ approved the writings in the Book of Enoch. Many of the early church forefathers supported the Enochian writings.

The Book of Jude in the New Testament even quotes the Book of Enoch. Although they were excluded as part of the canon of scriptures, they are widely used in the referenced work of Christian scholars. It aligns amazingly with the Book of Genesis and the intense spiritual conflict of that age. Sadly, Jewish scholars determined it was inconsistent with the Torah. It is one of the greatest influences concerning this topic and is a complete compliment to the Book of Genesis.

In his writings, Enoch writes in detail concerning the Days of Noah. He describes the angels as having violated both their own nature and position. He writes in details about the Great Flood and the terrible fall in his day. It may not be equated with scripture now, but it is a profound supplemental history that confirms Noah's time of darkness. The second portion of the book contains two visions. There is powerful information that is gleaned from the writings of Enoch. The evil activity of Satan's fallen angels is prevalent in his work. The spiritual pollution that is induced upon the earth at the time of the flood is specific and accurate concerning the generation of Noah.

It also verifies why the Lord had to go to the drastic measure of the flood to try to expel these hellish influences of the watchers that had contaminated humanity. Enoch was an awesome picture of a man of faith that used his gifts to further the Kingdom of God and bring glory to His name. His life reflects how God will deliver the faithful from the earth before the wrath of God is poured out in this final hour.

Prefacing for the Book of Enoch

Genesis 5

Enoch walked faithfully with God 300 years and had other sons and daughters. Altogether, Enoch lived a total of 365 years. Enoch walked faithfully with God; then he was no more, because God took him away.

Most believers have heard of Enoch from the Book of Genesis, but have little understanding of the importance and impact in history. Enoch is one of the only two who lived before the flood of whom was said to have "walked with God.". The name of Enoch comes from the Hebrew name "chinook," meaning "dedicated." In Genesis, this is the name that is confusing, because it is the name of both the son of Cain, and in contrast, the father of Methuselah. Enoch could not have come from a higher pedigree and the Bible confirms his amazing relationship with God and the validity of his writings as a scribe in Noah's day. Even the Book of Hebrews quotes that "he is the one that pleased God." His books and his witness are inspiration from the Lord, yet they have been neglected, because of religious dogma. His life set the precedence between the responsibility for coming Israel.

According to the past historic church, the Book of Enoch is not considered part of the biblical canon of scripture as it used to be by the Jews. Controversy arose defeating the validity of the writings of Enoch connecting the Old and New Testaments. Tertullian, being a prolific <u>early Christian</u> author from the early church in Rome, taught that the Book of

Enoch's prophecies were preserved by Noah in the ark, and that they continued and were read until the times of the apostles. But because they contained many famous testimonies concerning Jesus Christ, the Jews out of malice suppressed and abolished the whole book."

An erosion of Enoch's writings again took place at the hand of those establishing the canon of scripture of the New Testament as it was caught in the other writings of the apocryphal teachings. Christian churches still accept the Book of Enoch as having historical and theological significance, but they generally reject the Books of Enoch as non-canonical and part of the Apocrypha. Yet, the New Testament has explicit verification of Enoch in the Book of Hebrews and Jude.

We find in the Book of Jude a description of Enoch's ministry in Genesis. Enoch's faith compelled him to denounce the false teaching and ungodly living of his day, and prophesied the coming return and judgment by the Lord in the final hour before the flood. His writings are the deepest and most revealing light that defines the impact in the Days of Noah. I strongly encourage you to research these fascinating writings. There is a critical value of tying Enoch to the apostasy of today.

Jude's letter was famous for exposing the obscure and controversial points. Jude spoke of the angels who had sinned, who are now imprisoned and awaiting a future day of judgement. Jude proclaimed, "they were wandering stars, like comets streaking through the sky, these certain men astonished the world for a time, and then vanished into darkness. This was equated to the apostates of the nominal church that were already rising.

Jude intensely provoked the church to contend for the faith once for all delivered to the saints, including Enoch. There is a lot of earnest contention in the world but usually not for the right things. The faith once for all delivered to the saints is the primary worth contending for.

The apocryphal Book of Enoch describes the dramatic end of the fallen angels that left their first estate. Since the English translation found in Ethiopia in 1768, the Book of Enoch has made quite a stir in academic circles. It has been authenticated as existing and in wide use before the current church age. Many copies were discovered in 1948 in the Dead Sea Scrolls. This has caused many to wonder why it is no longer included in modern Bibles. Its accounts are identical in numbers of ways with the Book of Genesis. TJude leaves us with to "build yourselves up on your most holy faith." This means that we are responsible for our own spiritual growth and "snatching others out of the fire.".

The Contents of the Book of Enoch

The Book of Enoch as a collection of second century Jewish texts are succinctly attributed to Enoch, but there si grave ignorance of their validity and importance. As the great-grandfather of Noah, he was intimately connected with the anarchy that occurred from the heavens. Enoch describes the group of fallen "Watchers" mating with humans to produce a race of giants called "the Nephilim. The Book of Enoch can be read side by side with Genesis and you will find a mirrored reflection. For some, this book has created a phobia concerning the orthodoxy of scripture and at times an overreaction to its measure.

I encourage you to research these books and understand their history.

The Chronology of the Book of Enoch

- The Praise to God
- Hearing the Watchers
- The Messiah's Return
- The Indictment of the Watchers
- The Sins of the Watchers
- The Evil Results of the Watcher's Sin
- Their Betrayal and their Lawless Spells
- The Great Mysteries
- Enoch Speaks to Noah
- The Healing of the Earth
- The Destruction of the Giant
- Restoration of the Earth
- Enoch Communes with the Watchers
- The Evil Seed of the Watchers

The Confusion Today Over the Sons of God

2 Peter 2

For if God did not spare angels when they sinned, but sent them to hell, putting them in chains of darkness to be held for judgment; if he did not spare the ancient world Owhen he brought the flood on its ungodly people, but protected Noah, a preacher of righteousness, and seven others;

One of the most disputed terms through the church has been the validity of some of the terms in the Book of Genesis. There has been great debate over the identity of the "sons of God" that are in the sixth chapter of Genesis. After a thorough study it becomes evident that these are the fallen angels that have been in rebellion with Satan and came to pervert the ways of Noah's generation. It seems that this brings in the reason tat the Book of Enoch became one of the lost books of the Bible and the fantastic evidence of the full measure of the angelic rebellion. Many are phobic that the following topic is crossing the line. The fact is, it is these rebellious sons of God were the ones that had crossed the line. A major discrepancy within the theological community of Christianity in the past still exists over who the sons of God that are mentioned in the sixth chapter of Genesis. This clearly refers to the angelic sons of God that sexually abused the daughters of men. There have been several suggestions as to who the sons of God were that are illogical and contradict the references in the rest of the scripture. The children that were giants, termed the Nephilim could not be from human loins.

There are three primary views on the identity of these sons of God. The first is they were powerful human rulers, and the second is they were godly descendants of Seth, intermarrying with wicked descendants of Cain. The third we will discuss in the remainder of this chapter. There is a severe weakness in the first and second explanations that ordinary human males marrying ordinary human females does not account for why the offspring were "giants" or "heroes of old, men of renown." Furthermore, why would God decide to bring the flood on the earth when God had never forbidden powerful human males or descendants of Seth to marry

The Sobering Truth about the Sons of God

Genesis 6

When human beings began to increase in number on the earth and daughters were born to them, 2 the sons of God saw that the daughters of humans were beautiful, and they married any of them they chose. Then the Lord said, "My Spirit will not contend with humans forever, for they are mortal; their days will be a hundred and twenty years."

The third and only reasonable explanation is that these "sons of God" were the fallen angelic beings that had crossed the line of their first estate. They participated in obscene, perverse marriage with human females when they were not to marry and they were certainly not to have sexual relations in any form. In the Old Testament the phrase "sons of God" always referred to angels. It seems contradictory to say that angels are sexless and then to say that the "sons of God" were fallen angels who procreated with human females. However, while angels are spiritual beings, they often have appeared in human, physical form doing what humans do. The men of Sodom and Gomorrah wanted to have sex with the two angels who were with Lot. It is sensible that angels are not only capable of taking on human form, but are able of replicating human sexuality.

As to the specific sin of these angels, we are given the compounding facts in the Book of Jude and the Book of Second Peter. As in the case of Sodom and Gomorrah it was the sin of "fornication" and it means "going after strange flesh." Strange flesh means flesh of a different kind from the Greek word, "heteros". To commit this particularly repugnant sin, the angels had to abandon their own domain and invade a realm that was divinely forbidden to them by taking the daughters of men. The offspring of this union between the "sons of God" and the "daughters of men" was so extraordinary that it produced hybrid giants.

The interpretation of the sons of God in Genesis Six was never found to be humans before the fifth century A.D. We cannot deny the Jewish father's understanding of their own terminology. They invariably translated "sons of God" as "angels." The testimony of Josephus, the famous historian, is also of great importance. In his "Antiquities of the Jews," he confirmed the tradition of the fallen angels consorting with women of earth. He not only knew of the tradition but tells us how the children of such union possessed super human strength, and were known for their extreme wickedness.

Sometimes, the truth is stranger than fiction. The view that involves the fallen angels mating with human females has a strong contextual, grammatical, and historical basis. There is so much confirmation to this history, from many books of scripture to the compelling writings of Enoch that were extracted at that time.

This most tragic event went far deeper than realized. This rebellion of fallen angels that occurred in the Days of Noah was the complete counterfeit of a hybrid offspring that mocked of the prophetic incarnation of Christ through a virgin daughter of man, Mary. How perverted that Satan would inspire his seed of destruction by creating a counterfeit hybrid being through the daughters of men. At the fall of man, Eve was told that her seed would bring the coming Messiah, bringing salvation to mankind. As Satan always does, he uses mankind to produce his twisted image, instead of the image of God.

A sincere sidenote has to be the historic banishment of these hideous rebels that were chained in the abyss of Tarturas. In Revelation Nine, Abaddon is described as "the Destroyer," an angel from the Abyss who was king of a plague of locusts comes up from the abyss (the bottomless pit). It is apparent that God imprisoned the fallen angels who committed this evil sin, so that the other fallen angels would not do the same because of their extensive coverage in many areas that they did not adhere to. At the end of the Book of Revelation an authoritative angel comes down out of heaven, having the key to the Abyss holding a great chain in his hand, he seizes the dragon, the devil, and bounds him for the coming millennium. This is the present bottomless pit that incarcerates these wicked Watchers and a host of demons. Their abominable sin was so surreal and oppressive that the Lord brought great carnage and judgment, greater than what had ever done before. Evidently, the angels not only took on human form, but produced hybrid giant offspring that were pure evil.

❧ Chapter Seven ❧

The Truth About of the Watchers

Daniel 1

I saw in the visions of my head on my bed, and behold, a watcher, a sanctuary of heaven upon the earth and saw much bloodshed on the earth.

Enoch 6

You see what Asael has done, who has taught all iniquity on the earth, and has revealed the eternal mysteries that are in heaven, Then Michael and Sariel and Raphael and Gabriel looked down from the sanctuary of heaven upon the earth and saw much bloodshed on the earth. All the earth was filled with the godlessness and violence that had befallen it.

The fallen Watchers during the Days of Noah were seducing spirits that preyed on the human community in fatal ways. They taught forbidden knowledge and crafts that otherwise would have never been thought to develop, such as weaponry and sorcery. One of the greatest sins of the fallen watchers was their theft and betrayal of God to bring the secret arts and mysteries from heaven to the earth.

A frequent name and term for the angels in the Bible and almost an exclusive term in the Book of Enoch is the name, "the Watchers." In the Book of Daniel, there are three references to the varying classes of "watchers." The term is introduced by Nebuchadnezzar who says how in his dream that a "watcher" told of the prophecy that he would eat grass and go mad and that his punishment was "by the decree of the Watchers, the demand by the word of the Holy Ones." Enoch mentions the Watchers constantly and he even has a chapter called "the Book of the Watchers." These watcher angels were God's first celestial beings or "holy ones" who were to come down from heaven with authority to speak for God, but they left their first estate.

The Hebrew word "watcher" comes from the root word meaning "wakeful one or guardian." They are servants of God who "possess a joint authority to speak His decrees, and then act as divine messengers to bring devotion and revelation to human beings." According to the Book of Enoch, watchers can be either fallen angels or faithful holy angels. Holy watchers have always taken a particular interest in the earthly affairs of human beings, guarding them, and even interfering in or controlling situations that concern people. The list of damaging sorceries from the Way of Cain now preside grammatically in this final age. The list from drugs, witchcraft, technology and a myriad of demonic tools are now in fruition in the Mystery of Lawlessness.

In the Book of Enoch, the Watchers were initially sent to Earth to watch over humans, but who fell from grace and taught humans science and other skills: Here is a list of the leading ones.

- **Asael** taught all iniquities on the earth, and has revealed the eternal mysteries that are in heaven to progress the "Great Lie" that man could transcend into godhood with the secret tools that the Lord withheld from Adam.
- **Shemihazah** taught spells and the manipulation of plant life.
- **Hermani** taught sorcery for the loosing of spells and magic.
- **Kokabel** taught the signs of the stars.
- **Ziqel** taught the signs of the shooting stars.
- **Arteqoph** taught the signs of the earth.
- **Shamsiel** taught the signs of the sun.
- **Sahriel** taught the signs of the moon.
- **Asael** also taught men the technology to make swords of iron and weapons and shields and breastplates and every instrument of war to cause the horrible effects of tribalism.

As the Book of Genesis confirms, some of the archangels on high, looked down from the sanctuary of heaven upon the earth and saw massive bloodshed. The earth was filled with godless sorcery and violence from the Watchers influence. These Watchers were specifically forbidden and furthered the alienation from God captivating them into the occult. In natural and spiritual history, a society degenerates according to any invading influence. It goes from diminishing a God-centered spiritual life, to lawless liberalism, to finally seeking life's answers alien from God, and then to spiritism, couched in the occult. We have finally reached this final descent.

It is tragic that the Book of Enoch was discarded by default. The apocalyptic theme concerning Enoch's experiences with fallen angels, divine secrets, and the fate of the human soul after death, have left a gap for the answers desperately needed today. Messages about the angelic influences are more often distorted and Biblically illiterate even to the point of replacing them with the deception of extraterrestrials. Its various revelatory messages reflect the message of the Book of Genesis with precision, not the mindset of society over several centuries, that led to the doubts about its authenticity and authorship.

At this former time in the Days of Noah, the Watchers realized the depth of harm that they had caused humanity and sought out Enoch to intervene for them to the Lord. After Asael pleaded with Enoch for mercy from God, Enoch, told him, "You will have no peace. A great sentence has gone forth against you, to bind you. You will have no relief or petition, because of the unrighteous deeds that you revealed, and because of all the godless deeds and the unrighteousness and the sin that you revealed to humans."

Part of Enoch's mission was to pronounce God's judgment on the fallen watchers for creating the rebellion of humanity. The hope for an apocalyptic cleansing of evil for mankind was prominent in the Book of the Watchers, retelling of the deluge, when God commands the angel Michael to cleanse the earth from the torrid decadence. Although the fallen watchers began to fear God again, they had crossed an unforgivable line in a myriad of ways. Yet, there was never to be a reprieve for the fallen ones as the waters came to their eventual judgement into the bowels of hell.

The Fatal Tools of the Watchers

Jude 6

And the angels who did not keep their positions of authority but abandoned their proper dwelling. These he has kept in darkness, bound with everlasting chains for judgment on the great Day.

Enoch 12

Then the Lord said to me: Enoch, scribe of righteousness, go tell the Watchers of heaven, who have deserted the lofty sky, and their holy everlasting station, who have been polluted with women. And have done as the sons of men do, by taking to themselves wives, and who have been greatly corrupted on the earth.

In the Bible and the Book of Enoch, the Watchers were earthly shepherds of the first humans. It was their task from our beginning to just to observe and watch over the emerging human species to protect and serve. However, they were confined by the divine directive not to interfere in the ascent of humanity. Unfortunately, when the fallen Watchers arrived on earth, they decided to ignore God's command and defy his orders and became governors. There was devastating repercussions for both themselves and the culture.

As the remnant of rebellious watchers were seduced by the evil one, they began to capture and dominate the very ones that they were meant to protect. This assault evolved into grotesque proportions and all but the family of Noah were overwhelmed by this hideous invasion. The Book of Enoch describes the Watchers that were dispatched to the earth to continue to seduce and control the generation of Noah. We need to understand the progress of wickedness and corruption that was among the antediluvians and their facilitators. We must acquaint ourselves not merely with the sowing of evil but also with the nurturing, the growth, and the harvest of their sorcerous crop.

As Noah built the ark of salvation for him and his family, the rest of his generation partied in revelry and rioting until the day it began to rain. As the Watchers assaulted God's will, they taught humans various creative arts, valuable knowledge related to science and technology, agriculture, the use of cosmetics, metallurgy, medicine, astrology, and much more became a tragic gift. Unfortunately, the Watchers also taught humans how to engage in warfare. This corrupted mankind into greater violence and the thirst for power. This began the first world order through Cain and these angelic devils. We will delve into the progressive conspiracy of surviving the deluge and it fruition in the horrific first rebellion.

There is an innumerable amount of literature on this topic, but there is also a great deal of misinformation. It is incredible how much came from this historic original rebellion and how much of its articles somehow passed through the waters of the flood to the shores of a recovered earth. The seed of foundational empires and religious idolatry writhed from this time and were reseeded again by Nimrod at the city and Tower of Babel. This was the rudder of the evil advanced by these fallen creatures that continues to be woven in today's culture. We are the final manifestation of this dark past in the last global empire that would replicate the fall from the Days of Noah.

In summary, the Book of the Watchers contains five main threads regarding the sin of the angels that reflect earlier traditions.

Forbidden Knowledge of Make-up and Weapons:

The angel Asael descends to earth and teaches forbidden knowledge to women concerning female adornment, which facilitates lust. He showed them the art of making them: bracelets, and ornaments, and the art of making up the eyes and of beautifying the eyelids, and the most precious and choice stones, and all kinds of colored dyes. Asael also taught men to invoke warfare, and to make swords, daggers, shields, and breastplates.

Forbidden Knowledge: Magic and Spells:

In another thread woven into the story of the Watchers, humans are taught magic and other forbidden knowledge: They taught them charms and spells, and showed them the cutting of roots and trees morphing plant life for magic.

Forbidden Sexual Relations:

The sexual and spiritual relationships with fallen Watchers and the daughters of men became the greatest violation of these hideous rebels. This had immeasurable impact upon every facet of the society of Noah. This is currently occurring again, veiled in the occult, and poisoning our youth.

The Compounding of the "Great Lie.":

The fallen Watchers continued to teach humans that man could transcend into godhood with the secret tools that the Lord withheld from Adam.

The Teaching of Sorcery and Occultism:

Humans were subjected to astrology, conjuring spells, and the worship of creation rather than the Creator. This began to seed the twisted culture with godless philosophies that continue now on even a greater scale.

The Hideous Seduction of the Watchers

Genesis 6

When human beings began to increase in number on the earth and daughters were born to them, the sons of God saw that the daughters of humans were beautiful, and they married any of them they chose. Then the Lord said, "My Spirit will not contend with humans forever, for they are mortal, their days will be a hundred and twenty years.

Enoch 10

To Gabriel also the Lord said, go to the biters, to the reprobates, to the children of fornication; and destroy the children of fornication, the offspring of the Watchers, from among men; bring them forth, and excite them one against another. Let them perish by mutual slaughter; for length of days shall not be theirs.

The madness of this invasion exploded as it entered the realm of spiritual insanity as these angels left their first estate and begin to procreate with the daughters of men. The result of this illicit relationship between the Watchers and "the daughters of men" was the spawning of a monstrous hybrid race of warlike, cannibalistic giants called the Nephilim. This horrific sin is characterized in being similar in taking in young women by a form of rape through deception, although it is not clear that the women involved were innocent.

In the Days of Noah, nothing was out of bounds or labeled evil when temptation took over. The sexual and spiritual relationships with fallen angels were the greatest provocation of the Great Flood. I believe that this portion of scripture is denied, because it has been considered too hideous and unthinkable to embrace until now. This horrific account has been explained away by shallow excuses because it was the most sinful occurrence in human history.

This great sin of "the fallen ones" was Satan's first attempt to replace God as the image of man by preventing the "seed of the woman" that would deliver humanity foretold in Genesis. The assault was not only moral blasphemy but it distorted the physical makeup of God's boundaries and creation. The details of the last chapter give the basis for the demonic influences and schemes to harass and distort the human race.

We are told that the fallen angels that left their first estate and had sexual relations with females are now chained in darkness in the abyss until their full judgment. The influence of fallen angels today are through dark spiritual oppression upon the hearts and minds of the unbelieving and the systems of the world. Spiritism, occultism, political slander, and fleshly ways, are leading to this final rebellion. Seduction has opened the gates of astrology, extraterrestrials, magic, Wicca, and New Age perversion through which the evil spirits have captivated the minds and souls of men.

History gives us many avenues to research this age, but it should be done with great caution that it isn't conflict with the scripture. In Greek Mythology, the Titans were giants that came from the real account of the sons of God, "the fallen watchers" that abandoned heaven to live amongst mankind on earth. Angels appear naturally larger than humans especially in their natural spirit form but being made of supernatural force and energy, not of flesh and bone, they appear in various ways that they can be mistaken as humans.

If you look at the fruit of the present rebellion on earth today, there is no doubt that we are now facing the greatest spiritual deception and warfare that the earth has ever experienced. The influence of fallen angels and demons have returned, saturating culture in every category of society. Unfortunately, they are more glamorized than they are repulsed. With the increase of technology, it has given the ability to create art and entertainment to an incredible level laced with satanic leaven. It is ironic how many super heroes or arch villains have found their way into our minds. Hollywood, the drug scene, and other avenues have opened the door of sorcery and spiritism to the point it blurs the line between the physical and the spiritual.

The Hybrid Nephilim Giants

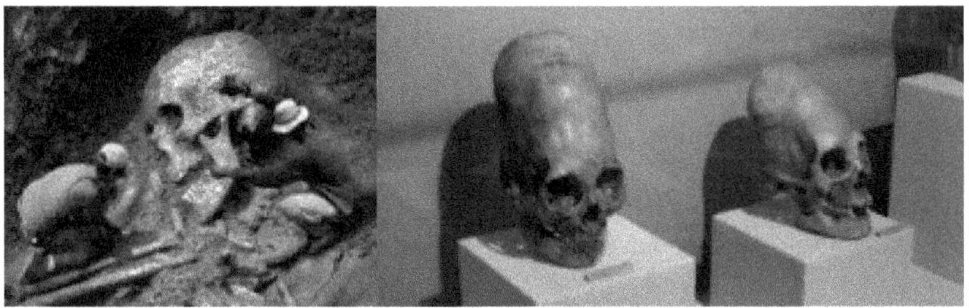

Genesis 6

There were giants on the earth in those days, and afterward, when the sons of God came in to the daughters of men and they bore children to them. Those were the mighty men who were of old, men of renown. Then the Lord saw that the wickedness of man was great in the earth, and that every intent of the thoughts of his heart was only evil continually. And the Lord was sorry that He had made man on the earth, and He was grieved in His heart. The Nephilim were on the earth in those days—and afterward—when the sons of God went to the daughters of humans and had children by them. They were the heroes of old, men of renown.

Enoch 15

And now, the giants, who are produced from the spirits and flesh, shall be called evil spirits upon the earth, and on the earth shall be their dwelling. Evil spirits have proceeded from their bodies; because they are born from men, from the holy Watchers is their beginning and primal origin; they shall be evil spirits on earth, and evil spirits shall they be called.

This historic holocaust and betrayal were concluded in the aggravated birth of the seed from hell. This incited a great deal of the historic mythology and was the direct influence of these hybrids, the Nephilim, and their fathers, the Watchers. In the Hebrew Bible and several non-canonical Jewish and early Christian writings, "Nephilim" means the seed of the fallen ones. The word "Nephilim" is translated as giants or Titans in some Bibles, and is left untranslated in others. This hybrid creature arose in the Days of Noah and they were brutal. They were a race of giants and super creatures who did acts of great evil. Their great size and power likely came from the mixture of demonic "DNA" with human genetics. The Book of Enoch, states that the Nephilim could no longer sustain themselves because of their enormous size, and began to consume men by eating their flesh and consuming their blood, as well as eating all the beasts of the Earth.

These beasts were called the "men of renown' or the "famous ones" which infers to examples given like Hercules and Atlas. Greek mythology was full of shadows of these giant hybrids. The Nephilim were also referred to as "Anakin," which means "warrior." Their destructive tendencies were a constant endangerment and perversion to humans, filling that generation with corruption and violence.

The remains of these evil creatures that have the appearance in odd ways to alien representation have been found all over the earth. They have no resemblance to humans or any other animal. How can contain genetic material "unknown in any human, primate or animal known so far?" So, are these Nephilim skulls? Do they come from a time in the world of Noah leaving a wonder of many people living today would ever dare to imagine? These skulls were discovered in the desert in an enormous graveyard that housed tombs packed full of beings with elongated skulls.

It is historic that after the flood, these demons again mated with human females, producing more Nephilim. When the Israelites spied out the land of Canaan, they reported back to Moses: "We saw the Nephilim there present during this time." While exploring the land that Israel was entering, the spies proclaimed that "We seemed like grasshoppers in our own eyes, and we looked the same to them." Their size and intimidation were like what they had never seen.

Whatever the case, these "giants" were destroyed by the Israelites during their invasion of Canaan and later in their history. Every facet of the apostasy of the Days of Noah is going to reoccur in a graphic way. There are reports of this despicable act but it is not yet obvious. We must keep our eyes and ears open to the winds that are blowing. This is the only symptom that is not blatant in these last days.

The Final Judgment of the Watchers

Jude 6

And the angels who did not keep their positions of authority but abandoned their proper dwelling, these he has kept in darkness, bound with everlasting chains for judgment on the great Day.

2 Peter 2

For if God did not spare angels when they sinned, but sent them to hell, putting them in chains of darkness to be held for judgment; if he did not spare the ancient world when he brought the flood on its ungodly people, but protected Noah, a preacher of righteousness, and seven others.

Enoch 17

And being numerous in appearance made men profane, and caused them to err; so that they sacrificed to devils as to gods. For in the great day there shall be a judgment, with which they shall be judged, until they are consumed; and their wives also shall be judged.

The fallen angels who produced the Nephilim were eventually cast into the Abyss of Tartarus into a place of "total darkness" in the center of the earth. Tartarus is described as a gloomy pit surrounded by a wall of bronze in the depth of eternal wrath. Along with chaos, earth, and eros, it was one of the first entities to exist in the universe. It is nothing less than a prison for the angelic Watchers that took wives in sexual perversion in the generation of Noah. This was not only the most grievous sin that these watchers could have committed, but they betrayed their God in every other way imaginable. They were the culprits that had raped the Lord's new creature that produced the seed of the global rebellion we are facing.

While Hades is the main realm of the dead in Greek mythology, Tartarus also contains numbers of villains. In early writings, it was primarily the prison for defeated gods. Titans were condemned to Tartarus after losing their battle against the Olympian gods. The word "Tartarus" is only found once in the Bible in the Book of Second Peter. This is defined as a pit of dense darkness where these evil ones are being chained and reserved for their final judgment. They are there awaiting their execution after their final rebellion in the Tribulation, yet they will be unleashed at the end of the Great Tribulation.

The idea behind the ancient word "lewdness" is sin that is practiced without shame, without any sense of conscience or decency. Usually, the word is used in the sense of sexual immorality. But it can also be used in the sense of brazen anti-biblical teaching, when the truth is denied and lies are taught without shame. In the Book of Jude, it had both ideas in mind here, because as the rest of the letter will develop, the spirits and certain men both had horrific moral defect.

In the Book of Enoch, the angel, Raguel was referred to as the archangel of justice, fairness, across Jewish and Christian traditions. Much like a sheriff, Raguel's purpose has always been to keep fallen angels and demons in check, delivering judgment upon any that over step their boundaries. These fallen Watchers will be held accountable for their continual dark rebellion. They will eventually share the eternal fire with their dark master, as God will wipe away all the tears that they have sown vengeance, and redemption.

The Book of Revelation has a reprieve for them to carry out a final act of war as they are released through the shaft of the abyss to torture the defiant human seed during the Great Tribulation. The earth becomes like the torment of hell as the predators are released to impale the earth with unspeakable deception and acts. They have been imprisoned for centuries and will take their vengeance on those remaining on the earth. They will continue to dispense their dark sorceries through these ugly remaining creatures. This is the place where it is speculated that Jesus went to preach when he spent three days and nights in the heart of the earth.

Before we forget, gratefully, most of the angels kept their faith in their Creator, kept their primary position, and protect us today as guardians. The final aspect of God's judgment upon these fallen creatures will be the loss of immortality, resulting in death like mortal humans. Though they were angels with divine immortality, they will reap the same reward of Adam and Eve in paradise, they will die like men and spend eternity in flames.

❦ Chapter Eight ❧

The Rising Cauldron of the Watchers

Encircling the Planet

1 John 5

We know that we are of God, and the whole world is encircled by the power of the evil one opposing God and His precepts

Cauldron: a large metal pot used in witchcraft to cast spells; a situation characterized by instability and strong emotions.

The angels in heaven were initiated in the beginning into the light and the love of God's heart. The Lord held back nothing from them and graced them with His wisdom and revelation in every facet. The Lord gave Lucifer and the hosts of heaven everything beneath His throne, yet after Satan's heart was filled with pride, he decided he wanted God's throne. Then a third of the angels conspired with him and stole these treasures to use them in sorcerous ways to continue their campaign. They stole the "secret knowledge" from heaven to manipulate and pervert humanity's rule of the new creation.

The Apostle John in one of his letters pronounced that the whole world was encircled by the evil one. This spoke of the spell Satan had cast to control and seduce God's new creature. The witchcraft and sorcery that was invoked through the Watchers was defined by the pentagram either right side up or upside down, to dispense good or evil. Sorcerers since the invasion have drawn a pentagram with a circle around it to manipulate a spell of influence over their target. This same craft is what the Prince of this World has done to vanquish our globe since their fall from heaven.

As we covered earlier, the Watchers dispensed their occult secrets in Noah's generation through the Way of Cain. This provoked the dissention against God's will and taught humans not only various creative arts, and the valuable knowledge related to science. The used metallurgy, medicine, astrology, and much more to establish their reign. This was the birthing the "cosmos," the new world systematized order that is the blueprint of Satan to derail the purpose of humanity even today. We travel this grazing maze treading the spiritual waters to stay above it through the Holy Spirit and the Word of God. The contaminating brew from the Watchers is now being poured out from the cup of the Harlot of Babylon and these birds of prey.

A cauldron was a witchcraft tool of cast-iron kettle that was used over an open fire. It is a vessel that transforms fragments of nature into powerful potions and spells. Cauldrons began production again in the early twelfth century and remained in use throughout all Northern Europe until the eighteenth century. Potters and brasiers, craftsmen accustomed to working with brass, manufactured these cauldrons. The cauldron symbolized many things, namely that "Divine Feminine," because it is viewed as the womb. This is related to creation, as in the womb of the earth. Cauldrons were of similar use as were the encircled pentagram in enforcing the sorcerer's will. These evil occult vessels were introduced in the Days of Noah as iron vessels for witchcraft and sorcery from the fallen Watchers. Today, there is little difference in the sorcery that is dispelled through crude practices.

The round shape and receptive properties of cauldrons make it sacred to the Earth Goddess, and it is associated with the element of water. However, given that the heat of a fire is necessary for much of the transformative work of a cauldron, some view it as sharing association with the elements of water and fire. Witchcraft is such a counterfeit and a twisted lie. It corrupts the spirit and soul of mankind away from the beautiful will of our Maker.

The Cauldron of the Occult

Deuteronomy 18

For example, never sacrifice your son or daughter as a burnt offering. And do not let your people practice fortune-telling, or use sorcery, or interpret omens, or engage in witchcraft.

The cauldron has made many appearances in mythology. One of the most famous mythological cauldrons, the Cauldron of Inspiration, was from the ancient Celtic goddess of rebirth, magic, and wisdom. When she attempts to give wisdom to her son, her apprentice is asked to stir the cauldron. Three drops fall onto his thumbs as he licks it off. He then becomes the underworld gremlin, Taliesin. The cauldron was supposedly a symbol of wisdom, and transformation. This is an example of the fallen evil prince of darkness mocking God. It is also the counterfeit to the inspiration of the Holy Spirit in every way.

It is bewildering to understand the variations and degrees of occultism that now cover the earth. They have all originated and digressed from the Days of Noah. They are all based on man reaching toward godhood through divination, selfism, and idolatry. It is futile and deceptive because our arms aren't that long. Only the eternal love of God reaching down to us through His Son is there no deceitful schemes or veiled motives. We are warned to be aware and educated concerning the devil's schemes.

The first excuse from Lucifer was to defame God and accuse him of not being protective, but just controlling. This now labels his true believers as blindly following ancient ways that are broad and bigoted. The truth is the narrow road to life is paved in the blood of our Redeemer. God's primary goal was to rescue us from sin and its instigator. A core belief of occultism is to deny the Lord of heaven be relabel by sin and "selfism," and to reject the thought of needing salvation. This other road is so broad that the masses can't even see its gate posts or the destination to lurking destruction. It has no restriction and touts as the satanic Bible "to do what you will." The early initiates of the Kabbalistic Mysteries believed that their principles were first taught by God to a school of his angels before the fall of man. There are volumes of distorted "secret knowledge" texts that are straight from the bowels of hell.

In Witchcraft traditions, the Watchers are not only the guardians of the portals to other realms, but are also the protectors of the magic circle, and witnesses to secret rites. Each of the ruling Watchers oversees a watchtower, which is now a portal marking one of the four quarters of the ritual circle. One of the goals of Satanists is to eventually have demonic spirits materialize in the guise of benevolent beings. They use rituals, dimensional portals, and blood sacrifice to make this happen. This is the same connection that was made by the Watchers in the Days of Noah.

There have been ages marked from the Days of Noah, but an unprecedented occult explosion occurred that is still continuing until the Day of Evil. Known as the era of free love, peace and awakening of the mind, the Sixties birthed what was known as the counterculture that revived occult mysticism. Breaking free from the suburban post-war monotony, the decade started a spiritual movement throughout the globe. The elixir of mystical religion, sexual revolution, darkening music and illicit drugs stole any innocence left from the war era. Before the Sixties, there had always existed a fascination with the occult and mysticism. Then then the so-called "ascending masters" influenced this renaissance of spirituality such as Helena Blavatsky, the founding mother of occult in America and Aleister Crowley termed, the beast.

Satan is the major influencer of ideology, perception, carnal desire, self determination that traps the masses. His influence also encompasses world philosophies, distorted education, and the thirst for power. The thoughts, ideas, and false religions of the world are under his control and have sprung from his lies and deception.

The pentagram is associated with neo-pagan religion; both white and black witchcraft. It is often depicted enclosed in a circle, a symbol known as a pentacle.

In these traditions the five points often represent the five elements of air, fire, water, earth, and spirit. It is rooted in deceptive carnality and invests in the temporal, rejecting God. When the Bible says Satan has power over the world, we must remember that God has given him domain over the unbelievers only by their consent. True believers are no longer under the rule of Satan, for the power of the evil one was disarmed at the cross. We are just passing through as ambassadors and eternal witnesses.

Luke 9

What good is it for someone to gain the whole world, and yet lose or forfeit their very self?

Since the Days of Noah, sorcery has enveloped the culture seducing the first distorted society from the fallen Watchers. This continues to this very day through a plethora of spells cast over unbelievers under the trance of "selfism." Enoch exposed in detail the craft of putting mankind under their control. This began the wicked perversion of sorcery drowning the planet with a chronology of tool that drowned the cultures of the empires from Babel.

Magic was invoked in many kinds of rituals and medical alchemy, and to counteract evil omens from the watchers. The ancient Mesopotamians believed that magic was the only viable defense against demons, ghosts, and evil sorcerers. They ancients also used magic intending to protect themselves from evil sorcerers who might place curses on them. Black magic as a category didn't exist in ancient Mesopotamia, and a person legitimately using magic to defend themselves against illegitimate magic. This is the heart and soul of the origin of Halloween or "hallowed evening."

The roots of European black witchcraft trace back when concepts of magic and religion were closely related, and culture closely integrated magic and supernatural beliefs. During the Middle Ages, accusations of heresy and devil worship grew more prevalent. The only major difference was the fact that curses were enacted in secret; whereas a defense against sowas conducted in the open, in front of an audience if possible.

This repeated through the ages to the crises of World War Two. Then, the possessed Adolph Hitler and the Third Reich became the last purely evil empire that clearly captivated the planet through sorcery until this final hour. In the Third Reich, Heinrich Himmler, was the false prophet under Adolph Hitler that authored the SS Occult Bureau that was built out of the SS radical wing of the Nazi Army. He leavened the drastic occult foundation upon the nation of Germany. In 1934, Himmler designed and implemented the Nazi Temple of Doom at Ebenholzkiste to as a New Global Religious Order to take the earth under the wings of the Third Reich from this evil dark fortress. Most people do not realize the ferocious undergirding of the occult as the core of this wicked movement. They also didn't see Hitler concealed in a dark room after mesmerizing a crowd frothing at the mouth.

Ironically, this matched in every way the fermenting New World Order of the Antichrist and the False Prophet, and it was the first regime that took claim to the name of the New World Order. Himmler strove to banish the roots of Judaism and Christendom from Germany to create a synthetic heritage based in the occult to verify the racist Aryan order. Himmler was also charged by Hitler to retrieve the Spear of Longinus which supposedly pierced the side of Christ, and the Holy Grail that was the chalice from which Jesus used at the Last Supper to serve wine. Hitler believed the possessors of these types of articles would rule the world. Following the method of the fallen Watchers, Hitler wanted these relics to manipulate what God had meant for good.

Another spiritual weapon that was used by Himmler was a cauldron tooled by the Nazi Otto Gahr, to falsify a genuine Celtic cauldron that was referred to as the "Goldkessel." They used it in their cultic SS rituals to cast his spells through demonic presence. During the final Nazi retreat, the cauldron was confirmed, and discovered hidden at the bottom of a lake. Aside from the broom and the wand, the cauldron is possibly the most iconic symbol of witchcraft in the imagery of popular culture. The origins of this association came to us from ancient Celtic myth, through cauldrons.

The Cauldron of the Sixties

Isaiah 47

"Go down, sit in the dust,

Virgin Daughter Babylon;

sit on the ground without a throne,

queen city of the Babylonians.

No more will you be called

tender or delicate.

Take millstones and grind flour;

take off your veil.

Lift up your skirts, bare your legs,

and wade through the streams.

Your nakedness will be exposed

and your shame uncovered.

It is critical that we understand that one of the most sorcerous times in history, a time that saw profound cultural and spiritual warping, was nowhere more intense than on the streets of **Haight-Ashbury in San Francisco**. This launched the era of free love, dropping out on acid and a new age. The truth is there was nothing new or free about it. It began a fatal descent that we never ever recovered from.

The idea of a stairway to heaven has been around since the Days of Noah. In the decade of the Sixties, we discovered a stairway to the abyss of Genesis. Music with drugs opened a "Pandora's Box" releasing hideous spirits that captured the minds of young people.

It is strange how Occultic Robert Plant of Led Zeppelin explained the writing of the most famous rock song, "Stairway to Heaven." Plant claims that something else was moving his pencil for him, leading him to speculate that Satan who was dictating the words, and along with the backward messaging, it possessed him. There was enough evidence for many listeners that the devil had his fingerprint` in creating this song. Plant had aligned with the dark occultist, Aleister Crowley.

Robert Plant was quoted, "this whole Led Zeppelin and the occult thing is important to me because the Zeppelin was my gateway into paganism. Jimmy Page's fascination with Aleister Crowley led Plant to want to know more about him and his sorcery. Robert Plant's interest in Celtic Mythology opened the door into the world of modern Witchcraft, and the ancient Druids, that were known for the sacrifice of their children.

The impact of Aleister Crowley on this band member replaced the religion of his family and his culture with a variety of extreme endeavors, from mountaineering to sex magic and all manner of practices derived from a synthesis of Eastern religions and the ancient occult. He eventually devolved further into the realm of black witchcraft. One of Crowley's ultimate dreams was to create a dimensional vortex that would bridge the gap between the world of the seen of and the unseen. He wanted a portal to the spirits on the other side. Later, we will look at the CERN project, determined to create a portal into the abyss of the next dimension. The other musical pagan priests as the Beatles, and the Doors broke the generation of the Sixties to the other side.

Hidden magic, astrology, and supernatural powers of the occult slithered its way into society with little notice. Just as terrifying is how many in today's culture consider the ancient elements of witchcraft the new normal. Other practices include horoscopes, fortune telling, contacting the dead, invoking spirits, Ouija boards, chakras, channeling energy, and incantations, among others. Sadly, each time you do witchcraft you are opening the doorway demonic spirits. Each spirit brings something to connect them within your spirit. to enslave you.

Technology has from the days of Noah to a become new highway for the "Sorcerer's Old Apprentice." From computers to space travel, our planet has been deluged with lying wonders for communication. and the doorways to torrid forms of sensuality have taken over. Every day, there is suspense over what will be next. It is the death blood of the systematized error. The cauldron of social media, Hollywood and television has cast a continual spell of selfism and sensuality. The mystical Harlot now spreads her false gospel that "sin is mythical" and life is only what you make it to be. Living for the moment by "eating, drinking and being merry" is the same mantra that was in the Days of Noah.

The systematized error is literally the progressive order that is consuming humanity as the global cauldron. It has forgotten God as it mocks him in defiance. Evil is now considered good as good is considered evil. The final generations have been taught the "Great Lie" from the serpent from Eden is the tree of knowledge that not only tastes good, but it transforms you into godhood. This is truly the final cauldron filled with the Mystery of Lawlessness.

Cauldrons were always used to provide dark mixtures of many contents to bring to power and initiate the evil prince's selfish, evil ways. As there has been an exponential increase of technology, the birth pains of "selfism" get deeper and more frequent. God's purpose for mankind wasn't to advance us as far as we can go or to know all we can discover, but rather that all should come to repentance and the knowledge of God. Ignorance in the carnal Days of Noah, and no repentance were the two destitute hallmarks of that generation.

The Cauldron of Worshipping the Earth and Stars

Isaiah 47

All the you have received has only worn you out!

Let your astrologers come forward,

those stargazers who make predictions month by month,

let them save you from what is coming upon you.

Surely, they are like stubble;

the fire will burn them up.

They cannot even save themselves

from the power of the flame.

The astrological beliefs between celestial observations and the terrestrial events have influenced various aspects of human history, including world-views, language and many elements of social culture. The term, "occult sciences" was coined in the late Middle Ages dating back to antiquity. Chief among these were alchemy and astrology, which included all things below the moon in the elemental world and all things above the moon in the super heavenly world. Linking these two worlds were the esoteric mathematics and geometry of Plato, which found a popular form in numerology. The Babylonian priest, Berossos, founded astrology and helped spread the zodiac in the Hellenistic world. These practices were sometimes connected with one another as intellectual magic, chiefly divination from the stars, they sought knowledge of fire, air, earth, and water. Because this kind of "natural magic" could be hard to distinguish from necromancy or the other "black arts," a separate entry is devoted to magic.

Earth-centered religion or nature worship is a system of religion based on the veneration of natural phenomena. It covers any religion that worships the earth, nature, or fertility deity, such as the various forms of goddess worship or matriarchal religion. Anyone who has studied the global environmental movement has no doubt heard of "Gaia." It is a revival of paganism that rejects Christianity, considers Christianity its biggest enemy, and views the Christian faith as its only "obstacle to a global religion centered on Gaia worship and the uniting of all life forms around the goddess of "Mother Earth." This cunning mixture of science, paganism, eastern mysticism, and feminism have made this pagan cult a growing threat to the Christian Church.

The idea of Earth as a living, divine spirit is not a new one. Plato said "We shall affirm that the cosmos, more than anything else, resembles most closely that living Creature of which all other living creatures, severally or genetically, are a portion; a living creature which is fairest of all and in ways most perfect." As today's version of paganism, Gaia is eagerly accepted by the new age movement and fits neatly into eastern mysticism, but science was needed to gather in the evolutionists and science-minded humanists.

A final strand of the rising unified global earth worship has recently come under the auspice and wings of the Roman Pope, and a core of godless interfaith children gathered at Mount Sinai. They joined in unity to erase the Ten Commandments with new ones under the name of "climate change." This grievous rebellion began an interfaith initiative connected to the United Nations to force the global government to accept the "New Ten Commandments." This will be detailed in my final book of this Exodus Trilogy in "The Sifting Blade of the Messiah. There is such an intricate web to the hour of trial we are in. There is far more to this story.

From the Cauldron to the Cup

The woman was dressed in purple and scarlet and was glittering with gold, precious stones, and pearls. She held a golden cup in her hand, filled with abominable things and the filth of her adulteries.

The Apostle Paul warned us that the rise of the Antichrist and the Mystery of Lawlessness will make a final entrance at the gate of the Tribulation. His appeal was first based on two facts: that day cannot be present without the presence of the great future rebellion that must come first before the second issue takes place. This rebellion is the sudden future and final revolt that provides the final seeding for the unveiling of the Antichrist. It is a system of cauldrons that are funneled and finally dispensed through the Harlot's cup of Babylon's toxin.

This brewing cup of poisonous betrayal has expanded to the point of becoming a pure cauldron of "Selfism." As the Harlot of Babylon is consumed in her adultery, she spreads herself and her elixir to the ends of the earth. The adulterous affair of empiricism and false religion dulled the hearts and minds of the gullible. This carnal delusion is founded in the shift from the acknowledgement of God as the center and replacing Him through the philosophy of selfism. They have been present or central at various times and in many diverse forms among cultures and religions worldwide, including both primitive and highly advanced cultures.

By drinking this cup, the inhabitants of earth become drunk to the sorcerous lie from the beginning, and do not know either where they are being led or what they are doing. This is a disorienting spirit that penetrates the masses with inverted vision. Today we must understand the potion of this cup and the misfortunes of those who drink of it in order to live without hope. It has streamed from the fallen ones and the Way of Cain to our penetrated borders.

The Cup of the Spiritual World Order

Revelation 17

The seven heads of the beast are seven mountains on which the woman sits. They are also seven kings. Five have fallen, one is, and the other has not yet come. And when he comes, he must continue a short time. And the ten horns which you saw on the beast, these will hate the harlot, make her desolate and naked, eat her flesh and burn her with fire. And the woman whom you saw is that great city which reigns over the kings of the earth."

The inconvenient truth is Satan is the ultimate source behind every false cult and world religion. Satan will do anything and everything in his power to oppose God and those who follow Him. The devil doesn't care how he gets commitment or worship because he has no integrity. He is the one who just wants to be in control, not to protect but to seduce. He is obsessed with taking from God what is His by any means through lawlessness and subtle slavery. He has used kings and kingdoms since the birth of the Way of Cain.

The final chapter of the cauldron of the evil one is currently being poured out upon the globe. This has been the cauldron of one empire and king being led by vicious, blood thirsty leaders in the extended adolescence of the e as aglobal village stemming from the Tower of Babel. The mile markers are closely behind us and all the signs before us all point to the new Babel and the final city of Rome with a Harlot providing her cup of intoxicants to the Antichrist and his ten kings. According to these veiled devilish prophets, this convergence will invoke the hellish earth pains, beginning with the false banner of universal peace from the new global war centered in the Middle East. The emerging global society will no longer be shackled to the truth and a Lord, as they choose destruction.

Every false religion in the world can be traced back to the age of Noah, from astrology to the Madonna and child represented by Nimrod and his mother. The Apostle John was astonished at the Mystery Harlot when her veneer was pulled away and she was exposed for who she is. It is a horror to see what she has become. She is mysterious because she is not who she appears to be. The nations are drunk on the wine of her fornication.

Revelation Seventeen gives the definition of a great religious Harlot in the final days that rides the Antichrist, the Beast of Revelation which we covered into the Tribulation. There has been great debate over this woman as far as her identity, her origin, and her purpose. There are definite similarities that have caused speculation in the past about who this Harlot is. Many find her to be a global religious system that is at the time of the end. That is just part of the truth. This Harlot has dispensed the wine of her fornication from betraying God through her chalice in the same occult practice of the Days of Noah.

Mystery Babylon awoke in God's glory but now she casts even a spell over herself in her dimming reign. She gloats as a queen and declares that she will see no suffering like the rest of the nations. She has grown to abhor the idea of the cross, sin and the need for redemption and she rules the world from a distance through her wealth and influence. She has learned to enslave the nations since her former days of serving them, and she is now reaping the whirlwind.

This Harlot has an arrogant spirit that has deceived her into thinking she still holds her former glory. She once was a cup in the hand of the Lord. Now she feeds her cup to the nations full of the sorcery derived from the Prince of Darkness. She has become spiritually inverted and she thrives on her sensuality and material wealth. Her new position takes on the character of Jezebel, a former pagan queen of Israel from Phoenicia. This ancient queen has been denounced as a murderer, prostitute and enemy of God, and her name has been adopted as the evilest woman in the Bible.

She sits on the throne consummated from the empirical ages and she is seducing the world through her sensual deception. She mocks her Christian heritage as she prostitutes herself for her own gain. Power and wealth have consumed her as she mesmerizes the world with her appearance and her intentions. She is gilded with all the beauty that the world has to offer, yet her soul is contaminated with her selfish desire.

This Harlot is clothed in purple and scarlet and she wears the color of royalty and the jewels of immeasurable wealth. She sits as a queen decked in gold and jewelry on her royal beast, yet who is she really? It is obvious that this Global Beast has the heads of former monarchs and kingdoms that have consented to their domination by this beautiful seductress. As a queen nation, she is used by the other nations under their king, the Antichrist who turns and devours her because he is ready to demand the worship of the masses to himself. Her claim to never see widowhood or to suffer is based on her arrogance that believes that neither God nor man will ever remove her from power or control her. She has misjudged God's patience that she will not suffer for her wicked and deceiving ways and that she is above everyone else. It is this final global regime. Now its evil conclusion the Mystery of Lawlessness is being poured from a cup, not a cauldron.

Four thousand years ago, we were warned through the prophet Daniel that the Babylonian empire that he was enslaved, was the beginning of a global empire that would web the earth into a world order that would be the throne for the Antichrist and his False Prophet. Bible prophecy foretold us of this fast-paced interconnected world order and its mushrooming advance in science and technology.

The Final Coming Lizard of Oz

2 Thessalonians 2

The coming of the lawless one will be in accordance with how Satan wonders that serve the lie, and all the ways that wickedness deceives those who are perishing. They perish because they refused to love the truth and so be saved. For this reason, God sends them a powerful delusion so that they will believe the lie 12 and so that all will be condemned who have not believed the truth but have delighted in wickedness.

The Wizard of Oz was a metaphor for the rising of populism and the fall of gold as the standard for wealth, representing the yellow brick road. The truth is, at the end of the road, the wizard they had sought had turned out to be a deceptive, impotent old man behind a curtain. This is being mocked at this very hour. This also reflects the road into the final globalist new order that would even deceive the very elect of God if it were possible.

As we have seen throughout time, Satan has always used his puppets to instill his evil will through empires and world religions. The lineage from Cain to the Antichrist has been the vein of destruction that he has inflamed and controlled the earth with. This is why he tempted Jesus in the desert with the kingdoms of this world. The Antichrist is the finality of kings because he becomes a hybrid, possessed by Satan, and this timeless renegade will finally demand the worship that is for God. This counterfeit Christ will mimic Jesus and proclaim his illusive Messianic image to the masses in Jerusalem, as they have been worn out by sequential warfare.

This imposter from hell proclaiming "peace and security" will take the stage in Jerusalem with lying signs and wonders enamoring every soul not hid under the wings of the Redeemer. This White Horseman of the Apocalypse gains control through the tactics of peace and power politics and by his charismatic personality and persuasive language. This coming world deceiver will be like previous dictators that have proven to be persuasive speakers, able to motivate the masses to their political ideology.

Like Adolf Hitler, who was able to mesmerize a whole nation by his inspiring speeches, the Antichrist will be no exception. He will then make a seven-year covenant of death and hell with Israel, pretending to give Israel protection in the land and settle the very volatile Middle East. He leads the horsemen of war, famine and death that help web the earth with his Mystery of Lawlessness. The earth will be desperate for the Messiah's return to rescue a faithful remnant and the lost nation of Israel in the Valley of Decision in Megiddo.

During the middle of the Great Tribulation, the Antichrist will receive a massive head wound and resurrect through the spirit of Satan. This final Cain, who is known in theology as the Antichrist, will be the one "who opposes and exalts himself above all that is called God so that he sits as God, showing himself that he is God." By this time, Mystery Babylon will have been destroyed by fire, and he will demand worship for himself alone. The Apostle Paul indicated that this Antichrist would not appear on the scene until someone "who now restrains" lawlessness and iniquity is removed. This person of the Holy Trinity who is restraining iniquity in the world today is the Holy Spirit.

The Word of God tells us that we will not know the hour or the day of Christ's return but we will know the season. Many believe that even the season of His return will be disguised, but that is not accurate according to the scripture. The same will be with the rise of the Antichrist. God will allow this great delusion to come to fruition as the world has rejected the clearest evidence of His will and higher authority. The Antichrist will purport the lie that he is "the Messiah" and he will call fire down from the sky on command.

The worldwide web that has been woven since the Days of Noah is nearly completed as the road from Oz. There is but one answer to the madness. It is by His Spirit and His Word. Having the mind of Christ means we embrace God's plan in this fallen world to bring glory and restore creation to its original splendor, to provide salvation through being a witness. It means we identify with His purpose "to seek and to save what is lost." The Holy Spirit indwells and enlightens the believer, infusing him with wisdom with the mind of Christ.

❧ Chapter Nine ❧

The Apocalyptic Days of Noah

Genesis 6

The Lord saw how great the wickedness of the human race had become on the earth and that every inclination of the thoughts of the human heart was only evil all the time. The Lord regretted that he had made human beings on the earth, and his heart was deeply troubled. So, the Lord said, "I will wipe from the face of the earth the human race I have created and with them the animals, the birds, and the creatures that move along the ground, for I regret that I have made them." But Noah found favor in the eyes of the Lord.

I caution you that you do not let yourself be frustrated by redundancy or drifting over the next two chapters. It is critical to understand the intricate linkage of the Days of Noah to this present evil age. We are to study to show ourselves approved. We are cautioned that we must hear things several times for it to register. Approval is not checking the box, but taking to heart and spirit a deep change from deep testing and deep truth. This issue to this generation cannot be overestimated.

It is devastating how far humanity has fallen since the Days of Noah. As the earth exploded in numbers, it had also exploded with rampant evil. Long forgotten was the righteous sacrifice of Abel. The tragic response was "the Lord saw that the wickedness of man was great in the earth, and that every intention of the thoughts of his heart was only evil continually." He turned to Noah as he found grace in the eyes of his Lord. Although the people of Noah's day were totally depraved, they were not the least bit concerned about it. They carried on the events of their fleshly lives without a single thought of God or His judgment. They had no fear and their conscience had been seared with the hot iron of indulgence. Does this sound familiar?

As mankind's identity faded from relationship with God, it adapted to the parasitical Way of Cain. The earth dimmed into the grip of "selfism" with a rampant thirst for more. Their hearts were hardened beyond recovery and their ears were dulled from the roar of rebellion. No one cared to seek God, and in turn no one cared to repent. You may still be asking, "why would a loving God go so far as to flood the earth and destroy most of His creation?" If we truly understood the degree of contamination that had occurred upon the earth, we would also grasp the present hour. The descendants of Cain had birthed the same apostasy that now floods our world today that we are accountable for.

To summarize, the devilish thread that was woven through the story of the watchers has woven the worldwide web of today. As humans were taught magic and the other forbidden knowledge, the increase the apostasy and delusion disarmed humanity from any glimmer of eternal purpose. The twisted watcher's ferocious desire to birth hybrid ephilim was to mock the divine infancy of the coming Messiah. The spiritual marriage with technology will finally come to pass with the coming image of the Beast with the "abomination of desolation."

Noah responded soberly to the birth pains that came upon his generation. His reationship with the Lord rooted and grounded his faith mightily as he stepped forward into his sobering mission. As the vine of rebellion had taken root, Noah understood the fatal flaw from Adam and Eve, had devastated the hour through the Way of Cain. This generation thought they were living normal lives during the time Noah lived, just before the Flood. God's grieving was not sorrow for making a mistake. God doesn't make mistakes. God gave His human creation the freedom to choose between right and wrong, as He was grieved in His heart. We will now cover twelve detailed causes that led to the Great Deluge with their progression that dominated the falling culture during the Days of Noah.

The Great Lie of Humanism

Romans 1

They exchanged the truth about God for a lie, and worshiped and served created things rather than the Creator—who is forever praised.

In the beginning, we covered how the possessed serpent in the Garden of Eden authored the potion of "selfism" that "you can be as god" that led to the great fall of man and the Way of Cain. To truly understand the outcome of the "Great Lie" from Genesis, we need to study the "Humanist Manifesto" that has saturated the global culture in its fruition today. It reveals the true fruit from the tree of knowledge of good and evil. It is the major intellectual movement that continued from the Renaissance, and then to the Age of Reason.

This began again in the late fourteenth century in Italy, where it matured, and spread through the rest of Europe, finding its home in our nation. The first Humanist Manifesto was drafted in 1933 at the University of Chicago. Many of the signatories were universalist religious leaders and men like Albert Einstein that acknowledged the existence of God but rejected Christ's divinity. The second manifesto in 1973 had hundreds of signers, many of them professors of religion and philosophy. The most recent manifesto was crafted and I do mean "crafted" by the American Humanist Association and served as a continuing goal and vision of the original Manifesto. These are the type of men that are described by the Apostle John as "antichrists."

Humanism is, at its core, the progressive philosophy declaring mankind as the heart of creation instead of the Creator. It leads to an amoral life of personal fulfillment without acknowledging God. It is guided by reason, inspired, and informed by personal experience to be the compass for life. Since the "Sixties, this sorcery has been morphed into a myriad of selfism philosophies. It is nothing less than the prideful delusion instigated by Satan with the original mantra of rebellion from the third heavens. This was rooted in Genesis by the tree of knowledge of good and evil (pleasure and pain in Hebrew). This is the spell that was cast from the beginning.

Here is the summary of this fallen final manifesto:

Knowledge of the world is derived only from observation, experimentation, and rational analysis for selfish gain.

- This knowledge as well as solving problems and developing technology is based on our intellect and our progression through human accomplishment. We recognize the value and progression in thought, the arts and our inner experience as a human soul making us subject to analysis and critical intelligence. It is completely devoid of spiritual revelation as a revived interest in the classical world and studies which focus devoid God, but on the lie of what it is to be human.

Humans are the integral part of nature, the result of unguided evolutionary change.

- Humanists recognize nature as self-existing with no thought of a Creator. They accept life by distinguishing things as carnal with no regard for an eternal existence. Imagination and perception are the rule of law. This is the heart of the Mystery of Lawlessness that revolutionized the Way of Cain.

Ethical values are derived from human need and interest that is tested by experience.

- Humanists ground their values in human welfare based on circumstances, interests, and concerns and extend it to the global ecosystem and beyond. Their eyes and their ears have become a god as they justify that the heart of man is the heart of God.

Humans are social by nature and try to find meaning in their relationships.

- Being accepted comes with our first breath. Humans long and strive toward a world of mutual care, free of cruelty and its consequences where differences are resolved cooperatively without resorting to violence, yet tribalism and violent corruption rules the day and the world order.

1 The Great Lie Manifested

Genesis 3

The woman said to the serpent, "We may eat fruit from the trees in the garden, but God did say, 'You must not eat fruit from the tree that is in the middle of the garden, and you must not touch it, or you will die.'" "You will not certainly die," the serpent said to the woman. "For God knows that when you eat from it your eyes will be opened, and you will be like God, knowing good and evil."

Sadly, even the deluge did not extinguish this hideous sorcerous lie as it is even more prevalent now. The main pillar of the "ancient mystery religions" was founded upon the serpent of Eden. This heresy came again at the Tower of Babel with the worship of Nimrod and his mother who was called the "mother of god." It has now manifested in so many ways in the global deception sweeping the earth. The Masonic author and Socialist, Edward Bellamy spoke of "the Ancient Mysteries" as the Masonic philosophy that celebrated the potentiality of God within each of us.

This fatal heresy is rooted in so many schemes across our planet. This is a frightening quote that exemplifies today's deception. "Caligula wished that the Roman people had but one neck that he might cut it off, and as I read this letter I am afraid that for a moment I was capable of wishing the same thing concerning the laboring class of America."

In western esoteric tradition, there is a concept of "as above, so below." This means that everything within the universe, depending on how you want to look at it is reflected within your soul because you have the world within yourself, you are the god within yourself. This is the great counterfeit of our spirit being filled by the Holy Spirit.

It is tragic that since our nation has strived to be politically correct, it has darkened the search for truth with a lawless permissiveness that is even defaming the general church. We are to contend for the faith and be able to answer every man according to the Word of God. There is a phenomenal spiritual deficit within our universities today. They are a microcosm of what may become of America. This form of moral and intellectual tyranny is peculiar to modern democracies, as French philosopher Alexis de Tocqueville observed a century long ago.

While yesteryear's tyrants employed force in their demand for outward conformity, modern democracy has "perfected even despotism itself" in its capacity to compel conformity of the mind and heart. As Solomon declared, "Man at his greatest estate is altogether vanity."

---

1 MYTHICAL HUMAN GODHOOD

After the rebellion of Lucifer and a third of the angels, these angelic renegades set their site on the first family in Eden through possessing the serpent and releasing the first lying assault upon humanity. Satan seduces Eve with the first two lies spoken to humankind, namely: "You shall not surely die," and "You will be like God." The lie of human divinity was the carrier that was the basis for the coming Way of Cain and the first rebellion.

---

2 The Bloodless Worship of Cain

Acts 28

Therefore, take heed to yourselves and to all the flock, over which the Holy Spirit has made you overseers, to shepherd the church of God which He purchased with his own blood. For I know this, that after my departure savage wolves will come in among you, not sparing the flock. Also, from among yourselves men will rise, speaking perverse things, to draw away disciples after themselves.

From the very beginning of human history, the key to salvation is revealed. When Adam and Eve sinned, God shed innocent blood in order to make their clothes from animal skins. This is the first picture of the covering of righteousness that we received when the Lord Jesus Christ died for us.

The Way of Cain's sinful life began when he refused the way of redemption and offered a bloodless sacrifice by his own hands. He embraced the lie that there is no sin, just diversions. Cain began the path of self-righteousness, refusing the consequences of his actions, then for the first time he shed blood. He arrogantly responded to that blood asking God, "Am I my brother's keeper." He then turned and blamed God for his actions. Cain rejected this blood and any accountability to God's will. Cain began the idea that man is without blame and needs no account for sin, that he was basically good. He believed that bloodless sacrifice and the works of his hand must be acknowledged by God or he would divorce him. How dare that his Creator would hold him accountable and correct his selfish endeavors.

What can you possibly offer God for acceptance concerning the way you have lived? The Apostle Paul said, "We shall all stand before the judgment seat of Christ, and that every one may receive according to the things he hath done in the body." The consequence of this is, that there is no creature which is not manifest in His sight, but all things are naked and open to the eyes of Him with whom we must stand. Without the blood of Christ, we perish in our sin. The Apostle Paul wept with tears over those who had become enemies of the cross and had made their senses their god. This was the solemn case of the generation of Noah. They refused God and refused to repent.

In the Old Testament the significance of blood in sacrifice was symbolic and represented life. It is the life blood of the animal that is to represent the atonement. With Jesus Christ, it is far more than symbolic. It is the pure devotion by God in His sacrificial death to atone for the sin and the weakness on our behalf of His prodigal children. The mockery of His loving sacrifice has reached a point of true desecration. With all of the mockery of sin, without the cross and the blood, there is no sacrifice for sin, but just a continuation. The final abomination of this is not the disobedience of the children of Israel sacrificing their children to Molech for selfism, but our hideous disobedience sacrificing our children for our convenience's sake.

Today we are repeating the history of Cain as we reject sin and deny our fallen condition. This generation is now cross-less and has rejected the only thing that can deliver us from ourselves. The Word of God and the Holy Spirit are the only antidote for the spiritual deception that has not only riddled our nation but even crept through the doors of the nominal church. World philosophy appeals to our pride rather than our desperate condition before God. If we do not realize our inherited condition, how can we escape if we neglect such a great salvation? If we reject the cross of Christ, we are left with no sacrifice for sin.

2 BLOODLESS SACRIFICES
Cain initiated the terrible doctrine that the sacrifice of redemptive blood was unnecessary. Cain rejected his sinful condition and instilled his prideful way to speak that our sin is mythical, and that we are on equal footing with our Creator.

3 The Rejection of God's Word and Authority

2 Timothy 4

Preach the word; be prepared in season and out of season; correct, rebuke and encourage—with great patience and careful instruction. For the time will come when people will not put up with sound doctrine. Instead, to suit their own desires, they will gather around them a great number of teachers to say what their itching ears want to hear. They will turn their ears away from the truth and turn aside to myths.

Cain rejected God's spoken Word and began an assault upon God's way and completely deviated from every principal he had been taught. He lived separate from God and created a godless society based on cities, government, economics, materialism, and spiritually morphed humanism that captivated the minds of men. His society shut the true God out of every facet of their culture. They slowly replaced God's Word and truth with a self-centered fabrication of life itself. This translated into the "Ancient Mysteries" that has swept through the ages into present day heresies and cults.

The Way of Cain despised God's authority because ``Cain wanted to be God just like Satan, his father. He rebuked not only God but every Word that came from His mouth. This set into motion the alienation from the Lord, and the wicked order that developed between him and the fallen watchers. This same rebellious spirit now possesses the global culture in an insolent way. Sadly, even our nation that has its constitution and laws based on Biblical mandate is now fading into secular humanism and political correctness. Most have no idea of the historical validation of the Bible and the incredible efforts from the past to keep it valid and translated from the original language. It is appalling how much this has even collapsed the moral fabric that once held us together throughout history. The decision that God is who we perceive Him to be or not to be is rampant and the refusal that truth comes in a variety of colors has stripped us of any spiritual equilibrium. Relativism and the rejection that there are no absolutes has paved the road again for the Way of Cain. When a society embraces a slippery slope of "truth," its foundation crumbles. A culture's attack on truth ultimately pollutes the culture itself with disfavor and unbelief. The generation of Noah pioneered this fatal apostasy as they proclaimed to be the center of the universe and we are continuing the rebellion through the final Mystery of Lawlessness.

3 REJECTING GOD'S WAY AND HIS WORSHIP
The Way of Cain rejected God's spoken Word and His way for mankind being valid. Cain rebelled and denied the sin that was crouched at his door and that he was accountable to God. Cain's greatest sin was not murder. It was betraying God. This led to His insipid thirst for power that was rooted in pride and selfish exaltation. As his father, the devil, Cain also desired a place above God.

4 Selfism Replaces the Worship of God

Jude 1

Woe to them! They have taken the way of Cain; they have rushed for profit into Balaam's error; they have been destroyed in Korah's rebellion.

In the beginning, relationship with God was the primary motivation for mankind along with relationships with our neighbors. The Way of Cain put Cain first and his neighbor's secondary in which they were there at his disposal. The progression of false self-deification and following other gods came next, which was prompted by fallen angelic influences that led the rebellion that God had to extinguish, if there were to be any hope for humanity.

Cain was not an atheist, but he led the future generations into denying the existence of God. Cain returned to the idea that blood and redemption were unnecessary because men were thought of as gods. Cain was offended at the accountability to his Creator or anyone else. His thirst to be supreme came from his evil conspirator, the Prince of this World. It is interesting how the Book of Jude marries Cain with ungodly people, who pervert the grace of our God into a license for immorality and they deny Jesus Christ, our only Sovereign Lord.

The relationship with fallen angels spread the lie from the garden to the entire culture. Noah's generation was seduced away from the simple and pure devotion that kept union with God. As Jesus warned in Matthew, that many will come and say that "I Am", the budding deception that "we are gods" took root in the last days before the flood and corrupted the minds of men.

There is now the surge to unite all religions under the banner of tolerance and the message that "all roads lead to God." This flies in the face of the heart of the Bible and rejects the truth that there is one mediator between God and man, which is Christ Jesus. While it is noble to respect each other's religious faith, the Bible teaches that the only way a person can be reconciled to God is on God's terms. All the others are man trying to reach godhood.

> **4 THE CANCER OF SELFISM (the Great Lie)**
> *Narcissistic selfism was the basic sin that began with Luciferic rebellion to ascend to God's throne. This heretical potion is even the mantra of the Satanic bible. "To do what you will" and to proclaim that "we are gods." It became the core of the Way of Cain that is the heart and soul of paganism.*

5 The Moral Inversion Seeded in Society

Galatians 5

Now the works of the flesh are evident: sexual immorality, impurity, sensuality, idolatry, sorcery, enmity, strife, jealousy, fits of anger, rivalries, dissensions, divisions, envy, drunkenness, orgies, and things like these. I warn you, as I warned you before, that those who do such things will not inherit the kingdom of God.

Satan is a sensual creature that preys on others through their senses. His attacks have always come from the lust of the eye, the lust of the flesh, and the pride of life. He works on the senses of our mortal flesh and spirit because he cannot influence the spirit born of faith by God's Spirit. He even tries to wear out the righteous seed by exhausting them, both physically and emotionally. He knew God's plan from the beginning, and that His law of procreation requires everything bring forth of its own kind. Yet, Satan determined to build his own kingdom by hybridizing humanity. By sexual lust, he mingled the sons of God with the daughters of men, to mock God's way. Through intermarriage, those in Cain's line were bastardized by corruption and violence to partner with the fallen Watchers to subdue the earth in the apostasy.

Through the bait of temptation, the devil can destroy lives and families and society. It is however important to realize that while the devil can tempt, he cannot force anyone to engage in an act of immorality. In other words, whether one will commit a sin does not depend on the devil. It depends on the attitude of the one tempted. Without boundaries and the power of God's Spirit we are dead in the water to temptation. James cautions us "Therefore submit to God. Resist the devil and he will flee from you."

> ## 5 Moral inversion Replaces God's Law
> *Idolatry is the core of immorality and the essence of the pride from evil. The essence of the pride of life is anything that exalts us above our godly purpose and offers the illusion of God-like qualities, wherein we boast in arrogance and worldly conceit. When we lose faith in God as our foundation, we are susceptible to all temptation and immorality.*

6 The Seeds of Sorcery

Deuteronomy 18

"There shall not be found among you, anyone who practices divination or tells fortunes or interprets omens, or a sorcerer or a charmer or a medium or a necromancer or one who inquires of the dead.

The term "goetia" finds its origins in the Greek word "to go", which originally invoked diviners, magicians, healers, and seers. Initially, Grimoires, also known as "books of spells" served as instructional manuals for various magical endeavors. They cover crafting magical objects, casting spells, performing divination, and summoning supernatural entities like angels, spirits, deities, and demons. Although the term "grimoire" originates from Europe, similar magical texts have been found in diverse cultures across the world. It now covers the planet as a "new gospel.

Sorcery is clearly sinful and is not to be part of the Christian life. James warns us that there is a wisdom that is "earthly, unspiritual, that is of the devil." This is what sorcery offers. Sorcery was one of the vicious articles that God wanted to extinguish by the flood. Tragically, sorcery resurrected through Nimrod at the Tower of Babel, and continues as a river from hell today. In the above scripture, we begin with a people that have gathered to make a city, and a tower. These people set out to make a name for themselves, and the tower they were going to make was to reach into heaven, and to ascend above God's throne as Lucifer originally proclaimed. Many occultists declare that when man is filled with pride, and has accumulating a vast amount of knowledge and metaphysical input, he will rule and reign.

In the Days of Noah, sorcery and magic was partitioned by the Watchers, and given out to seduce the gullible. This helped bring order for the purposes of bringing the masses into their rebellion, extending the battle against God. However, the Watchers did not look upon humans fondly. Watchers sought to dominate them into submission; their Nephilim offspring even cannibalized them. Contrary to common belief, the magic of the Watchers did not belong just to them. They stole it from heaven to weaponize it to conquer the planet. Such knowledge and power, was to morph humanity under the spell of the evil one.

It is shuddering how the word for sorcery in Greek, "phamekia" is where we attained the word, "pharmaceuticals," is devouring this generation through drugs. The greatest cause of death in males between fifteen and forty is the new fascination with fentanyl. The hope for an apocalyptic cleansing of evil was prominent in in Enoch's, "Book of the Watchers," God commands the angel Michael to cleanse the earth with the Flood, Enoch uses descriptions that are usually reserved for the end-time, the prophets, and the Book of Revelation. He has a vision that will soon be fulfilled when all the earth will be cleansed of evil and wickedness.

> ## 6 THE IMPACT OF SORCERY
> *Sorcery is an attempt to bypass God's wisdom and power and give glory to Satan. God has no tolerance for sorcery. Sorcery is listed among the sinful practices of the nations.*

7 The Corruption Seeded in Society

Genesis 17

Now, God saw that the earth had become corrupt and was filled with violence. God observed all this corruption in the world, for everyone on earth was corrupt.

The Bible describes sinful humanity as corrupt: "the fool says in his heart, "there is no God." They are corrupt, their deeds are vile; there is no one who does good. The Lord looks down from heaven on all mankind to see if there are any who understand, any who seek God.

All have turned away, all have become corrupt; there is no one who does good, not even one." Sin is like the cancer of the human soul. It often starts unnoticed, as a small compromise. There may be a few infectious symptoms, but we dismiss them as due to some other problem. But the cancer is there and growing, working corruption in the individual and tainting his relationships. If unchecked, it contaminates an entire society.

Jesus warned that the people of Noah's day ignored God's cautions and ignored Him. They went about the normal things of life, oblivious to the repeated warnings of judgment, until it was too late. This means more than the total corruption of our nature, and refers to its universal dominance. The seed of relativism testifies that there is no truth or reality. It is so bold that it declares that perception is reality, and basically, we are our own gods.

It is becoming increasingly obvious that to understand what the world was like in the Days of Noah, we only need to watch the daily news. It grieves God tremendously to see rebellion and sin, and He only brings judgment after He has repeatedly warned and appealed to us to turn from our sin. When He does judge, His judgments are always just. It means that despite the corruption, the horrible violence, immorality and degradation around Noah, God's grace for the individual still shines through.

The intervention with sorcery and technology was bad enough but the moral infection brought the Lord no choice than to deluge the planet. By the time of Noah, the infection of the hidden ways of the watchers and the inbred Way of Cain brought utter darkness and selfism to rule the planet. The option of man repenting and turning back to God's way had been totally swallowed up over a hundred and twenty years. We will cover this extensively in the following chapters.

> **7 Corruption leavens the Days of Noah**
> *Noah's day was a time of unparalleled corruption with people going on about life without any regard for God. They did what was right in their own eyes, that led them to death. They created the first universal prevalence of open daring sin, and rebellion against God with no reprieve.*

8 The Violence Seeded in Society

Genesis 6

Now, God saw that the earth had become corrupt and was filled with violence. God observed all this corruption in the world, for everyone on earth was corrupt.

There is another factor that concedes to total corruption. The violence in this context is more than the unavoidable warfare that arises between human beings. It is the malicious, oppressive violence that anyone would recognize as sorcerous and sinful. It is interesting to note that Jewish interpreters in the past have believed that this violence or lawlessness arose from too much ease and affluence. These people had everything that they wanted and consequently had to invent new types of distractions through tribalism. They lived with no thought of God or their fellow man. How sad that the lie from the serpent robbed them of everything that mattered or that had eternal value.

Violence is always birthed from rebellion and "selfism," but is rooted in the pain of living in past wounds. It is a collision of refusing the will of God and reaping the consequences. Working with gang kids, I learned they thought their lives were based on the perception of territory and respect. They honestly had neither. Their territory was an illusion and their respect was based on our father and no father. The reverse is a generation drowning in the sorcery of drugs as they tread the deluge in this present evil age.

If we create an environment that caters to evil thoughts, sexual immorality, coveting, wickedness, sensuality, pride, and foolishness, we cannot be surprised if murder pops its head up too. That is exactly what happened when Cain enveloped himself in his own way. If we legalize the rest of the list, regulate it, and condone it, we cannot be surprised that we can suppress evil thoughts that express themselves in murder. Violence was a great inheritance of man from the fallen Watchers and their seed. In violent warfare, they were aggressive to bring the earth under the banner of a unified force to conquer the planet.

8 The Perpetual Seeds of Violence

God hates violence. Ironically, the Hebrew word is Hamas, meaning wrong, cruelty, malicious injustice, or sinful violence. God's view of it is made clear in the fact that he overthrew the evil society of Noah's day because of their wickedness. Noah's culture was characterized by a debased mind, and all manner of unrighteousness, murder, maliciousness, heartlessness, and ruthlessness. The violence was an outworking of a debased mind.

9 The Birth of Lawlessness through Cain

Proverbs 11

The Lord detests those whose hearts are perverse, but he delights in those whose ways are blameless. Be sure of this: The wicked will not go unpunished, but those who are righteous will go free.

Satan has used two basic venues in his assault upon humanity. The first is annihilation and the second is to embrace as many as possible through deception and seduction by spells. This breeds an altered state of consciousness which leads us into a dark hall of confusion. He is the author of confusion that cast heavily upon the generation of Noah. The Way of Cain is mysterious to even many Christians today. It is evident that it had profound impact upon the Days of Noah. Once again, we need to understand the fruits in these times to grasp the importance.

The Mystery of Lawlessness was Satan's secret plan to ruin humanity through seduction as he conspired with the fallen angels. It has always been the antithesis of God's mysterious redemptive plan. This mystery, seeded in the Way of Cain has expounded covering the field that Jesus parabled with the "wheat and the tares. The Apostle Paul described the "lawless one" as a false worker of iniquity through lying wonders, fueled by the power of Satan. This concedes to the success of his apostate rebellion, for he finds many who are eager to believe his lies.

The word for mystery in Greek, "musterion" is in something into which one must be initiated, instructed, before it can be known, something of itself not obvious and above human insight. It is hidden and veiled to the innocent. It now possesses the heart of mankind in a global parameter. This sorcery is dispersed through the godlessness of our age through media, politics and especially through errant religions just as it did through the Way of Cain. This spirit of "selfism" is the soul of the Way of Cain and the tragic triumph of the current Mystery of Lawlessness. It infected every life before the deluge, but the remnant of Noah. Life can be so unpredictable. When times are good, it can feel easier. But when times feel difficult, it is even more important to trust God. God's unchanging character can give us a firm foundation when things feel unsteady and uncertain.

10 The Techno-Explosion from the Way of Cain

Daniel 12

But you, Daniel, keep this prophecy a secret; seal up the book until the time of the end, when many will rush here and there, and knowledge will increase."

The Book of Genesis and the Book of Daniel have given us a comprehensive list of the mechanical arts that morphed those living in the Days of Noah. It helped transfer the masses into worshipping the creation rather than the Creator. The secret art of technology rendered humans to avoid any remainder of the curse that produced an alienation from the Creator. In Genesis Three, we see humanity rejecting God's good purpose for life that brought a curse on creation.

Sadly, the fallen angels brought their secret mystic tools to induce the power and medium to the rebellious cause of the Way of Cain. Ironically, an example is God using the atom to create yet man used it as a vehicle to destroy through the ultimate bomb. First and foremost, technology is undoubtedly and constantly necessary in our lives, but it is easily abused. We appear to be developed, but the truth is, we are less and less evolved. That is why the total dependence on technology is would destroy us in the end without the intervention of our Messiah. The basic principle which we need to understand, when thinking about technology is this: technology by itself is what we call "amoral." It is neither overwhelmingly good nor inherently evil. Like lots of things in this world it's something with great power for good but which is also deeply affected by the fall and the susceptible heart of man.

The generation of Noah was the first apprentice of Satan to what the future would hold. The use of mankind's tools of the Watchers made an indulgent society thinking they had no use for God. Interestingly, Noah used the same technology to build the ark. Most do not realize the incredible advance of technology from Cain's expulsion to the building of the ark. The size of the ark is estimated to have been nearly six hundred feet long, being as long as two football fields. It was over ninety feet wide with a height almost sixty feet. There is an argument made that Noah may have had access to more sophisticated technology than we have today. We don't know how ancient people built many of the stone structures in South America or even the remarkably constructed Egyptian pyramids. The ancients obviously had a technology we just aren't aware of. There is always speculation of extra-terrestrials imprint, but the Watchers defined this way.

The generation of Noah was the first apprentice of Satan to what the future would hold. The use of mankind's tools of the Watchers made an indulgent society thinking they had no use for God. Interestingly, Noah used the same technology to build the ark. Most do not realize the incredible advance of technology from Cain's expulsion to the building of the ark. The size of the ark is estimated to have been nearly six hundred feet long, being as long as two football fields. It was over ninety feet wide with a height almost sixty feet. There are a myriad of questions concerning technology through history. We don't know how ancient people built many of the stone structures in South America or even the remarkably constructed Egyptian pyramids. The ancients obviously had a greater technology than we are aware of. The building of the ark is just one other example oof the seeds of technology.

From the prophet Daniel, we were warned that his book would be opened with the birth pains of technology that would explode in every aspect of a global culture. In the times of Daniel, information came only orally or hand written. Daniel warns the culmination climaxes in the second half of the Tribulation as the Antichrist lassoes humanity with the climatic technology that will bring the "Mark of the Beast. Everyday there is an onslaught of the techno-explosion surfacing rendering life so easily indulgent, captivating and enslaving the earth.

10 The Line of Cain Births Technology
The invention of the mechanical arts through the invasion of the Watchers began a crusade from the Prince of this World eventually leading us to the Valley of Megiddo. Technology was stolen by Satan from the third heavens and was released them to Cain to begin the separation between God and humanity. Tnis is at the center of the present culture.

11 The Cities of Cain

Genesis 4

Cain made love to his wife, and she became pregnant and gave birth to Enoch. Cain was then building a city, and he named it after his son Enoch.

Cain was the originator of cities and its foreign culture, void of God as its center. With those cities came the increase in the mechanical arts, weaponry, and the arts. The fundamental ideas behind cities included the specialization of labor, a system of laws and government, and artistic development. Everything we have covered so far were the fruit from these cities. Instead of God's inspiration, the Way of Cain led these cities through the watchers' inventions of the mechanical art. A society of self-sufficiency, far away from God's security began what would entrap mankind throughout history.

Warfare led to conquering smaller kingdoms, and then powerful states and nations with rulers began. This began the worship of men of renown and the total forgetfulness of the one Creator. False gods were created to meet the needs of the lost and a system of idolatry arose out of the new pagan societies. One city after another was built leading to the destiny of the city of Babel with its tower of self-worship. The web of order had the blood of technology and the bodies of cities and nations to further the evil will of the Prince of this World.

With the Garden of Eden in Genesis, life proceeded to the ending with the city of New Jerusalem in the Book of Revelation. The biblical story reveals how God has been working throughout history to establish a city filled with his glorious presence. This further suggested God's original goal was to dwell with his people in a holy city.

The city of Enoch was the result of Cain's efforts to find a way around the curse the Lord had pronounced on him. Since the ground would no longer yield crops, he and his descendants turned to livestock for their sustenance, wearing their skins and eating their meat, and began to gather in cities for protection. Unregenerate Cain exalted himself in defiance of his God. The most tragic aspect of Cain's descendants was that they grew to accept "the lie from the Garden of Eden," that it was all about them.

The seeds of Cain's cities from Genesis have ripened into a final web of delusion of kings and empires that eventually lead to the final Babylon and the Antichrist. The heartbeat from the Way of Cain is now pulsing through the Babylonian system that is being globalized today. God revealed in the Books of Daniel and Revelation, the world- ruling Gentile empires that would exist from the time of Babylon's empire to the Second Coming of Jesus. This covers a span of more than 2,600 years. Globalization pretends to hold an answer to the world's financial troubles, among other things. However, prayerful consideration and research reveals disturbing historical precedence through the history of progress.

12 The Road to Globalism

2 Corinthians 1 8

For such people are false apostles, deceitful workers, masquerading as apostles of Christ. And no wonder, for Satan himself masquerades as an angel of light. It is not surprising, then, if his servants also masquerade as servants of righteousness. Their end will be what their actions deserve.

World History has been built on the shoulders of world empires that have been in revolt against the King of Kings and His purpose since the very beginning. The travesties of the world wars are an example of great change that fermented a techno-explosion that completely morphed life as we knew it. With the advent of television, the internet and the computer it has opened a 'Pandora's Box" of technology to help implement the final New World Order. Emerging philosophies and the refining of imploding "selfism" have blanketed the planet with the merging spiritual unity that will eventually permeate the souls of men with another gospel under the False Prophet.

The emerging global economy married to global politics has shifted the power and wealth to a rising secret government. The hidden agenda of the United Nations is vilifying Israel and any true spiritual foundation. National borders are being dissolved as the planet is melting into a collusion of globalism. The shift is taking place from a national to a global network by a godless insurrection to bring forth a system that will overwhelm the masses and enthrone the Antichrist through the Mystery of Lawlessness.

This spiritual deception is now being activated through social engineering and *global* political control. Satan delights in deception and using false light into camouflaging his real intentions of perverting God's eternal will. He will romance you with a gift only to enslave you in its idolatrous habitation. The evil one has used religion and world empires as his Trojan horse since the erection of the Tower of Babel.

There is an unmeasured crisis taking place concerning where the so-called "Global Reset" is catalyzing the New World Order in the culture everywhere. People around the world are beginning to lose hope that their leaders can solve these ever-growing problems. Yet there is hope, but those things hoped for only come after a traumatic downfall. The world is about to begin experiencing the worst times of suffering and destruction it has ever known. The Greek word, "cosmos" means "systematized error" which is the system of evil devised by Satan. It is the course of this age streaming of confusion through kingdoms, and fallen kings.

Here is some of the framework that the world order has derived from.

Social / Cultural Schemes

- The line of Cain created a society mingled with the arts and social interaction separated from godly principles. Luxury and refined culture, a love of the arts and music became a part of Cain's way. Hedonism and humanism became the lifeblood of the civilization of the line of Cain. The basis of morality was as decadent as the fallen angels that led them into deception.

Government Systems

- Cain birthed the structure of cities that began the path for national control and eventually to fallen global systems. These systems that took root at Babel, continue in the global Babylonian system of today. The interpretation of the dream of Nebuchadnezzar gave us a blueprint of kingdoms that would lead to the rise of the Final World Order. The dream statue of Nebuchadnezzar gave us the vision that the world empires or orders would produce a multiple empire integrated into a ten-region global entity. We are at an unbelievable point where the globalist agenda is spreading like wildfire in the mysterious circles of power as the economy broadens globally.

Economic Control

- Agriculture, seafaring, the wheel, metallurgy, and myriads of inventions brought in trade and exchange in a social market. This began the structure for what is in existence in our global economy of today. The expansion of communication has brought this to a fever pitch. The internet, computers, and a myriad of technical advances has exploded the global network as it has shrunken the planet.

Military Power

- The birth of weaponry began with the line of Cain and thirst for control and territory birthed the need for warriors and weaponry. The history of warfare has had a plethora of destructive impacts upon mankind since the days of Cain. The further along we progressed in the art of weaponry, the graver the consequences have become. The Book of Mathew reminded us that the increase of war would be a major sign of the last days. Warfare has been a constant through time and it ends in the Valley of Megiddo when Christ returns to save His remnant from the clutches of the Antichrist.

Evolving Tribalism

- The more we have shrunk the earth through technology and global communication, the more fractured we have become in politics, culture, racism, family structure and relationship and communication. As we are warned, the final global union will be like iron mixed with clay which can never be cohesive. It is fascinating how the more the United Nations stretches toward peace and unity, the more opposed it remains. From racism to gangs, the tribal impact continues to rise and grow from the least to the greatest.

๑ Chapter Ten ๑

As in These Days of Noah

Matthew 24

But about that day or hour no one knows, not even the angels in heaven, the Son, but only the Father. As it was in the days of Noah, so it will be the coming of the Son of Man.

There is an ancient Native American story that tells of a wolf being hunted down by a wise old hunter. In hist tent, he was not wanting to have direct confrontation with the dangerous creature so he chose another path. The hunter stayed in his tent and thickly coated the blade of a sharp knife in blood trusting in the wolf's ferocious appetite for blood.

He then took the knife outside and jammed it in the snow upside down. As the wolf came upon the frozen blood-soaked knife, he began licking the blade over and over trying to satisfy his appetite. Eventually, it became a flowing fountain, until he collapsed on it and died. The wolf thought that he was eating from a fountain of blood, when in truth, he was drinking his own blood. This is a sobering parable of the ravenous addiction of man for the schemes of the Prince of Darkness in the Day of Evil. The swirling

123

rebellion separating God from His creation has reached fruition in every nation upon the earth.

The planned deception from the Prince of this World has woven a fatal matrix to destroy humanity in its fall since the Days of Noah. As we trace the stream of history from the origin at Eden to the despotic time and destruction of the flood, we see the clear bloody fingerprints of the satanic rebellion that has stained the globe.

Tragically, within the last generation the seeds of rebellion that provoked the flood have returned like weeds in a garden. Christ warned us that the fruition of the Way of Cain would not just be present, but in full force at the time of His return. Many do not understand that now is the season of retribution as we are swallowed up by the fermenting global carnival of deception.

The twin inversions of the Way of Cain, followed by the Mystery of Lawlessness have swept the earth, twice as a spiritual deluge that is drowns humanity in a continual tsunami that ascends from the bowels of hell. The birth pains now are contracting and the repeat of the Days of Noah are now descending as the masses ignore the darkened clouds on the horizon. They continually mock the promised return of the Messiah, and worship the moment. We have forgotten who died for us, as we re-crucify Him in our life as our nation is free falling into the new generation of Noah.

In the last chapter, we had investigated the seeds that were planted by the Way of Cain that come to fruition in the Mystery of Lawlessness that ushers in the Antichrist. The twelve symptomatic marks of the Days of Noah in the last chapter are now in full bloom as we face the coming of Jesus Christ. We are told in scripture that the end would climax like birth pains to a woman. The rebirth of Israel has spun the prophetic time clock out of control.

The birth pains of history have greatly deepened and so have the satanic assaults swaying humanity's devotion to the god of selfism. Satan's ultimate strategy in conquering planet earth will be to eventually possess the Antichrist and use the new world system of today to entrap mankind into worshipping him and destroying the remnant of Israel. The New World Order will have implemented the fullness of all his developed schemes and have captured the minds of men into thinking in his selfish, prideful ways to bring this delusion of "selfism" to fruition.

1 The Fruition of Mythical Godhood

Genesis 3

"You won't die!" the serpent replied to the woman. "God knows that your eyes will be opened as soon as you eat it, and you will be like God, knowing both good and evil.

Unity is like free will. It can be a great blessing or a horrid curse, depending on its usage. Jesus never coexisted with contradictory claims to truth, even with the Pharisees. If Jesus had been content with co-existence, he could have even escaped crucifixion. We should live peaceably with all people, but we must not reduce peace to a glib assertion that all paths lead to God. The assertion that all faiths are the same and there is no exclusive truth is a great stumbling block, and one that excludes all but the universalist. It represents an incoherent quest for tolerance and has arrived as a "cancel culture.

The real danger of the philosophy to just coexist is its underlying assumption that how we live is ultimately a matter of human logic, not spiritual reality. The lessons of history make clear that we will never achieve peace and harmony by compromising truth. The purpose of life is determined from beyond humanity. Co-existence treats Jesus Christ merely as an important moral teacher and disregards that he revealed himself as God and reduces the saving act of God to a set of rules. It claims that if we live in a certain way, we will attain salvation.

Man's quest for his own version of truth and self-divinity, has historically not only denied Biblical truth, but it has turned us inward, instead of upward for godly wisdom. The evolution of the age-old Lie of the Devil, "Yes, hath God said..." has given birth to our modern age brand

125

of humanism, which rules as the "false religion" of the world. This heresy that has been known in theology as the Antichrist spirit, is the one "who opposes and exalts himself above all that is called God or that is worshiped, so that he sits as God in the temple of God, showing himself that he is God."

Equally amazing to the doctrine of the Trinity is the doctrine of the Incarnation. The miracle of Jesus Christ being born of a virgin, comprising both God and man, confounded even the pharisees. The plurality of persons within the unity of God, and the union of the Godhead into manhood in the person of Jesus was the ultimate mystery and the ultimate gift. Tragically, Satan always takes the most precious things of God and mocks and distorts them. The births of the Nephilim were Satan's ultimate sin and mockery of Christ

This is the brass ring the serpent has longed for since the creation of humanity. The Bible prophecies the Antichrist will supersede all forms of religion and demand worship for himself alone to attain this. The most popular apostasy today is the teaching that God has revealed himself in many ways through different cultures proclaiming all religion are from the same God with different names and many interpretations. The toxic conclusion is that there are many paths to Godhood, which has caused the destruction of many. This has stained even the mind of many passive Christians today in the name of unity and permissiveness.

The one-world religion described in Revelation Seventeen will be part of the end-times scenario. The term Harlot is used throughout the Old Testament as a metaphor for false religion. She is a political, economic titan nation with a cup of sorcery that intoxicates the earth. The actual identity and makeup of this inclusive religion has been debated for centuries. There is no doubt that a one-world religion under the False Prophet will be a part of the Tribulation, perhaps made up of numbers of different religions, sects, and isms that are bound together like iron and clay. The alliances forged by the False Prophet will unite church and state as never before. At the Harlot nation's demise, the Antichrist Beast of the other nations will consume her with fire, because he alone will demand all worship for himself as he even demands marking humanity for this desperate attempt to steal man from the Lord. The unthinkable judgements will begin. The two remaining empires will be sifted for their idolatry and sorcery because they refused to repent.

2 The Fruition of Bloodless Justification

2 Corinthians 11

Today I promised you as a pure bride to one husband, Christ. But I fear that somehow your pure and undivided devotion to Christ will be corrupted, just as Eve was deceived by the cunning ways of the serpent. You happily put up with whatever anyone tells you, even if they preach a different Jesus than the one we preach, or a different kind of Spirit than the one you received, or a different kind of gospel

The reality of the blood of Christ, the Messiah as the symbol for atonement for sin originated in the Old Testament. The shadow was that once a year, the high priest made an offering of blood on the altar of the temple for the sins of the people. "In fact, the law requires that nearly everything be cleansed with blood, and without the shedding of blood there was no forgiveness." But this blood offering was a shadow of Christ, the Messiah, had to but it had been offered again and again. This was a foreshadowing of the "once for all" sacrifice which Jesus offered on the cross. While the blood of bulls and goats were a "reminder" of sin, "the blood of Christ, a lamb without blemish or defect," paid in full the debt of sin that we owe to God, and we need no further sacrifices for sin.

As we have seen, the Book of Hebrews proclaims "how shall we escape if we neglect such a great salvation." It also testifies that without the shedding of blood, there is no sacrifice for sin. Almost every world religion has no concept or understanding of original sin and the need for a ransom. It is based on the spiritual evolution of man becoming a god. His cleansing blood as a perfected lamb is the only gate back to right standing with God. The two basic eternal impacts of the cross are the forgiveness of Christ and the release of his empowerment through the Holy Spirit. This was only possible through the blood of the cross. Our world today is in total darkness when it comes to the revelation of Jesus Christ. The idea that he was just a man or a prophet extracts the power and purpose for why He came.

In George Barna's "Top Trends," the statistics show that just twenty per cent of Christians say they live in a way that makes them dependent upon God. Sadly, a similar percentage of Christians claim that the most important decision they have ever made was to invite Jesus Christ to forgive them and be their Savior. And just one-sixth of Christians say they are totally committed to engaging in personal spiritual development. The tragedy is that these statistics reflect those that are supposed to be believers in our nation. If these statistics are true about today's believer, what about the unbeliever?

3 The Final Eclipse of the Word of Truth

2 Timothy 4

In the presence of God and of Christ Jesus, who will judge the living and the dead, and in view of his appearing and his kingdom, I give you this charge: Preach the word; be prepared in season and out of season; correct, rebuke and encourage, with great patience and careful instruction. For the time will come when people will not put up with sound doctrine. Instead, to suit their own desires, they will gather around them a great number of teachers to say what their itching ears want to hear. They will turn their ears away from the truth and turn aside to myths.

Rejecting the Word of God is to reject God Himself. He is the living Word and without the inspiration of the Bible we will die in our sin. We are warned by the Apostle Paul that in the last days that truth and purpose in life founded upon Biblical principle will erode into lawlessness against Godly mandate and create a total global rebellion that will replicate the Way of Cain and the Days of Noah. Eternal truth is released through God's impending Word. Any other foundation has no power to forgive sin or release God's transforming truth.

Our nation in the last century has slowly drifted from our original Biblical foundation and our Judeo-Christian base creating the church and state separation metamorphosis. Our Christian heritage has been stripped away and has replaced faith in God with a secular humanistic foundation. There are three places young people ultimately learn and develop their worldview and belief system. In the past, these were school, church, and home. Education has diluted into godlessness and selfism, Input about spiritual meaning has been totally restricted. Church has been abandoned by young people, and faded into passivity, while most homes have devolved in so many ways, because God is no longer the center and heart of the home. Sadly, technology and media took over, and have saturated youth, and distorted communication and relationships at every level.

The foundation of the Word of God has been abandoned for another gospel, as our culture now replicates the Days of Noah. The shift in Europe has even been far worse with the Bible labeled as mythic, errant, and unreliable. Most church building have been renovated into bars and restaurant. Tenets of the faith will once again have been exchanged for selfism and idolatrous perceptions. An idol is anything that is above God in your life. This emanates the overwhelming philosophy of relativism, that truth, and morality exists in relation to culture, society, or historical context, and is not absolute. Essentially, relativism says that anything goes, because life is meaningless.

The skyrocketing global unbelief is awakening the Antichrist spirit that is now smothering the planet. The great falling away, which is well under way in our day, is not an event which has taken place in a short time. The absence of a Biblical foundation has now been replaced by false teachings which have been fed slowly to the masses. The great falling away has been a progressive apostasy as in the Days of Noah, and it is affecting everyone except the very elect of God. Our nation's rock bed of scriptural validity has been decimated since the last World War. Our moral fabric has torn from every seam from the raging lawlessness of the impending last days.

Statistics by George Barna show that the percentage of teens that embrace salvation, that believe in the Bible and have orthodox Biblical views has fallen from ten per cent to only four per cent today. There are exploding numbers of teenagers who accept moral relativism and pluralistic theology as their foundation of faith, if they even have a faith. The sad reason is that only nine per cent of adults in our nation have a biblical worldview. Other bewildering statistics by Barna tell us that forty-three per cent of Americans said it doesn't matter what religious faith you follow because they all teach the same lessons. The most frightening statistic reports that only half of the country's Protestant pastors, fifty-one have a Biblical worldview.

4 The Cosmic Selfism in the Last Days

2 Thessalonians 2

And with all the deceit of unrighteousness in those who perish, because they received not the love of the truth, that they might be saved. And for this cause God, all send them strong delusion, that they should believe a lie, that they all might be damned who believed not the truth, but had pleasure in unrighteousness.

Selfishness is at the core of apostasy in every age and in every rebellion that has occurred on the globe. It is always sparked by a narcissistic leader that contrives an initial ascension. This last rebellion has been just the opposite. It has been introduced through a global deception that the Antichrist will quickly step into and bring to fruition. The global communication network with so many veins, has immersed this generation with sensual and selfish appetites.

The great deception of selfism has manifested in a far greater way than I could have ever imagine before. It creeps its way through this age and will completely surface as it finally introduces the revelation of the Antichrist. This deception cuts to the core of life and purpose in general and specific. It is narcissistic in its inception and it is gilded with angelic beauty as the Harlot of Babylon. In fact, it is the toxin in her cup that has intoxicated the masses with her deadly potion. The nations are drunk on the madness that "we are gods" and it is all about us. The love of many has already grown cold as we were forewarned and the belief in the mysteries of old, are now being fed to the masses with a sugar coating. The sorceries of Hollywood, drugs, and social media are seducing the global culture in a way that has never been witnessed since the Days of Noah. The saddest dilemma is the person in the pulpit preaching that God is our "sugar daddy" to give us our heart's desire.

The paradigm of Mystery Babylon is reaching its final level. The political, spiritual, and economic web of globalism has encompassed planet earth and readied her for the evil prince of this world. The spiritual core of this deception is the "I Am" teaching that enshrouds most world religions. These basic self-based religions are about evolving into godhood. These dogmas reject the divinity of Christ and His Holiness as they trust the darkness that is within them. They deny their own sinful depravity and declare as Lucifer that they are the reason for their perceived brightness.

Selfism in today's world has mutated into present day relativism. It is the polarization of absolutes. Barna finds that most of the youth of today find the absolutes defined in the Bible as closed-minded and bigoted. They feel that you have your own personal code and it is truth to you and others create their own truth. This is the New Age mantra that has permeated the global culture.

The Word of God warns us that 'what seems right to man in his own eyes will lead him to death. Most at the present are willing to make changes, if the pathway promises benefit and enjoyment, and generally avoids pain, conflict, and sacrifice. This same delusion is also at the roots of the secret orders of Masonry, the Illuminati, and the basic New World Order. It is found in almost every nation on the earth except the destitute remnant that is striving to survive.

The Bible is very clear that this powerful delusion has slowly grown through the ages and climaxes at the rise of the Antichrist. This will be the platform for the "man of lawlessness" to stand on to bring humanity to its final descent. Few understand the spiritual intoxication that this brings even to the point that this evil counterfeit will appear to be the global "Messiah" to save the world. He will take his seat in the global center of Jerusalem, claiming his deity and world power.

5 The Amoral Invasion of the Global Culture

2 Timothy 3

But mark this: There will be terrible times in the last days. People will be lovers of themselves, lovers of money, boastful, proud, abusive, disobedience to parents, ungrateful, unholy, without love, unforgiving, slanderous, without self-control, brutal, not lovers of the good, treacherous, rash, conceited, lovers of pleasure rather than lovers of God, having a form of godliness but denying its power.

Many years ago, a scientist did an experiment where he took a pair of ordinary glasses and replaced the lenses with inverted glass. He walked around seeing upside down for two weeks, stumbling until he adapted to his new perception. When he took them off, he stumbled around again for two weeks. This is what the spell of being self-centered, not God centered has done to this generation.

Cain seeded this moral decadence beginning with murder, and then conspired with the fallen Watchers to create the first godless society. The continued fall began at the Tower of Babel to Babylon. The freefall of spiritual godlessness with congruent empires grew as the line of Abraham progressed alongside until the birth of Christ. We now sit on the precipice of the last global empire, and the final Harlot of Babylon that is falling, becoming the cage for every foul bird.

Moral code began to devolve through the Mystery of Lawlessness over the centuries by idolatrous empires with the early climax of Rome, as Judaism fell under idolatry and refused to be the Light to the nations. Pagan, godless philosophies seeded through the Way of Cain began to take root from philosophers like Confucius, Aristotle, and others. They continued the ancient humanist philosophy leading to today's selfism. The moral theory of Aristotle, like that of Plato, focused on the virtuous way of life by its relation to happiness. Beginning in the seventeenth century, the Age of Reason, ironically termed the Age of Enlightenment was an intellectual and philosophical movement that began dominating Europe with global influences and effects. It included a range of ideas centered on the value of human happiness, the pursuit of knowledge obtained by means of reason and the evidence of the senses. Voltaire, Rousseau, and Nietzsche, arguably the most influential shapers and explorers of the moral and cultural fall from a Christian foundation. Rousseau focused on the growing inequality of modern society and the hypocrisy of believers in God, the unity of selfism, and the loss of civic virtue.

Then, Frederick Nietzsche declared a false democratic equality. He identified with Rousseau about the loss of individual and cultural greatness. However, Rousseau and Nietzsche were more than mere critics; they both put forward powerful alternative visions of how we ought to live. They focused specifically on their views of selfism and its realization. It focuses upon the modern self's desire to be a god, while facing the ethical responsibility of integrating the world. Tragically, this was a period where these humanist philosophies assaulted Christianity in the name of logic, and provoked Deism, the belief in the existence of a creator who does not intervene in the universe. One of its main intentions was to destroy institutionalized religion and the legitimacy of the Bible.

With the rise and fall of the "Sixties," the wheels came off with the ferocious prophetic whirlwind of drugs, the occult and rampant atheism. Spiraling through the Sixties, there was an incredible spiritual demise where we are seeing every prophetic sign bursting forth across the globe. It became a schizophrenic phase of exploration and indulgence. The Sixties became a collage of personal and cultural exploits, most that turned the heart of man ice cold toward God and one another. It ushered in the Mystery of Lawlessness that the Apostle Paul warned would complete the fatal Way of Cain. With the journey to the moon, the lancing of racial tensions, the challenge of stagnant politics and apostate religion sadly seeded the great deception and the numbness that would eventually deeply mark the age.

For some, it was the defined dawning of a spiritual New Age. Madame Blavatsky introduced a greater fall that began in the nineteenth century with theosophy. It teaches that the purpose of human life is spiritual emancipation, and claims that the human soul undergoes reincarnation upon bodily death according to a process of karma. It promoted universal brotherhood and social evolution, although it does not even have a moral code.

It is the thought of evolving into God, straight from the serpent in the Garden of Eden. Sadly, rising in the twentieth century, the New Age movement, marrying the spread through the occult and metaphysical religious communities. It looked forward to coming to the "New Age" of love and light and offered a foretaste of the coming era of godhood. As we witness the downward spiral of our society today, we realize that the warning of the last days has come to fruition. When we view the descending moral values in our nation, the divorce rate, out of control abortion, pornography, drug addiction and child abuse.

6 The Fruition of Cultural Sorcery

2 Peter 3

Most importantly, I want to remind you that in the last days scoffers will come, mocking the truth, and following their own desires.

The above scripture from Peter summarizes the rise of scoffers at the very end that will "mock the truth" by turning to the senses. The word mock means to "ridicule by counterfeit." Paul wept over these enemies of the cross whose god had become their senses. He also warned, "Do not be deceived: God cannot be mocked, a man reaps what he sows." The grave problem is the nominal church hasn't rushed towards the gates of the consummation of all things, but has chosen to run along-side the edge.

In the Sixties, a new spiritual and nature focused religion started to gain steam. It was deemed, "wicca," but it was the original practice of witchcraft, and the white side of the occult. Its followers were called "wiccans." For people on the outside looking in, there was the possibility for some confusion on what, exactly, wiccans practiced, including how it related to paganism. The enemy doesn't stop trying to lure us, and our families, back into the darkness because we have chosen Christ. So, it should come as no surprise that we must be prepared to face an enemy that wants to harm us.

In the following decades there has been a steady rise in interest and practice of the occult, especially among the young. For example, on the social media platform TikTok, there is a large increase in people posting videos under the hashtag '#witch Tok', and interest in new age ideas such as "manifesting which can lead to demonic possession." There is also an increasing interest in tarot cards, seances, fortune telling and a myriad of occult influences. Children's cartoons and some Disney movies are laced with humanistic witchcraft. Harry Potter movies have seduced even believers into discounting the influences that are drowning our kids. This trend has been attributed to the decline of interest of youth in traditional Christianity. In an article entitled "Witchcraft is the perfect religion for liberal millennials," the author claims: while some churches shame deviant sexuality, witches believe that all types of sexuality should be cultivated and celebrated so that women rise from the influence.

Today, the greatest form of sorcery is drug abuse. The Bible translates the Greek word, "pharmekia" or "witchcraft." Sorcery is described as bring an altered state of reality, and opening the door to the spiritual. Drugs back then were mainly used by witches and sorcerers. Drugs were most used in pagan worship to hallucinate and to try to get in touch with evil spirits. Drug use has been termed as "the lazy man's sorcery. It is tragic how many young people have lost their soul or their lives to drug use. Today, the number one killer of males from fifteen to forty-five is fentanyl.

7 The Fruition of Corruption in Our Society

Revelation 19

His judgments are true and just. He has punished the great prostitute who corrupted the earth with her immorality. He has avenged the murder of his servants."

It is overwhelming to consider the corruption that is taking place in every nation spiritually and politically today. The global mandate is being built on human reasoning symbolized by the tree of knowledge of good and evil. Corrupt government are seducing the people they are meant to serve, corporations are fleecing the economy at the expense of those they are supposed to serve. This even goes down to the corruption in the pulpit that is fleecing their flock. Sadly, our nation promotes selfism and the worship of today's idols in the perverse global system. Sin and greed inevitably bring its own punishment, and there are always consequences to disobedience. Thus, when we go into captivity in these last days, it is because we speak of God, but are heart is far from Him.

The Greek word for world, "cosmos," is defined as the systematized error that is fully in force like never before. It cuts across and into all races, religions, and cultures. It is the future that is mocking the truth and God Himself. The issue of idolatry comes to the forefront in the Book of Revelation in response to the outcome of the sounding of the sixth trumpet. For the remaining two-thirds of humanity not killed by the plagues, they "did not repent of the works of their hands, so as to not worship demons and idols of gold and silver and bronze and stone and wood, which are not able to see nor hear nor walk." Many idols today are still wood, stone or metal in the forms of cars, houses, and many forms of higher desires.

8 The Fruition of Violence in Our Society

Psalm 58

No! You plot injustice in your hearts. You spread violence throughout the land.

I used to watch the show, "Law and Order." It always begins with a homicide or violent crime. At four years old, my youngest son loved to sit in my lap. One day after watching a murder with a gun on the show, he got down and went to his room. He came back with his toy gun he had gotten for his birthday. He placed it on my lap and said, "Daddy, take this, it can put evil in my heart. Talk about "out of the mouths of babes." I was stunned and ashamed of how ignorant I was about what this truly meant. I have never forgotten it.

Violence is a not just a social and political problem, it is rooted in the spiritual realm. The violent murder of Cain authored the violence from the original sin of pride. It served no useful purpose, but was an ambiguous expression of impotence and dominance. It manifested jealousy from a tainted heart that refused even God's authority as the sin that was crouched at his door overtook his soul. At once, Cain's self-image of what he wanted others to believe him to be was exposed. As Jeremiah said, "The heart of man is deceitful above all things, and desperately wicked: who can understand it? Cain was the author of human violence as we face its fruitful climax .in this final hour.

It's hard to believe that every time we hear about another mass shooting that nothing was able to prevent it. Rather it be a result of international terrorism or through the hands of a neighbor, the tentacles of violence are webbed throughout the globe, married to a heart of corruption and merciless tribalism down to the tormented soul. The wounded are always the one that will wound others but there are countless triggers throughout society.

Our global culture is permeated with activities which glorify blood and violence. From the movies we watch, to the books we read, to the nightly news, blood and violence are everywhere. Individuals are both repelled and attracted to it. Much like straining to see the damage a car wreck has done. For all the protest over the amount of violence people are exposed to daily, these shows, books, or movies are among the most consumed forms of entertainment. Popular culture gives a person insight into the underlying beliefs of a society. It seems that as blood is a measure of life, those violent acts which are most bloody are the most compelling, they are saturated with glamour, because they are a combination of fearful threat and its potential loss.

Jesus warned us that through the Beginning of Sorrows that the escalation of war will increase exponentially, and that nation will rise against nation. This is different because it is rooted in the Greek word, ethnos," meaning ethnicity. This is about the battle between skin color, the violence from gangs to gender war and family disputes. The enemy will dissect us in any way that he can.

9 The Fruition of the Global Cities of Babylon

Revelation 18

Then a mighty angel picked up a boulder the size of a large millstone and threw it into the sea, and said: "With such violence the great city of Babylon will be thrown down, never to be found again.

The Way of Cain set up the world system through the birth of cities and society. It then evolved into world empires and is now leading us into a global empire made of many pieces. Cities have always been the engine for cultural change and the core for government and intellectual perception. Since Babel, they were the power center until the creation of broader government. The previous topics we have covered all found their nest in the city. The city of Rome became the pinnacle of ancient cities with streets, market places, arenas, parks and even a sewage system. It also became the core of the most blasphemous society in existence. By modern times, cities began to canvas society and find the fruition point with the Industrial Revolution. This led even the United States to leave their farms in droves looking for an easier and more indulgent life.

Cities became very attractive places because they offered people not only work but also many things they can do in their free time. A multitude of stores and activities gave pleasure and recreation to fill the time that became available. As with the cities of Cain, evil has thrived greatly in the cities around the world. Since the Second World War, the great apostasy began to ferment in the cities around the globe.

The worship of God began to fade and be replaced by selfism which began to explode and find its ignition in the Sixties. Unfortunately, gangs, drugs, sexual promiscuity, and violence all found their breeding ground in cities. Material and hedonism swept the earth leaving little thought to eternal matters. Cities often are the devil's workshop for causing a temporal distortion of life and intent. The advantage that cities provide can bring carnality to come to our fingertips. The direction of our present global society is graphic and dark. For centuries now we have been heading towards globalization of the world based on secular values. Especially in the last century, our planet is being founded on the elimination of all traditional values, especially Christian values. This is because the true spiritual values set by Christ are polarized against today's new secular beliefs. This spiritual apostasy is now global eradicating the traditional Christian world view across the earth. This has led us into the jaws of lawlessness and soon the Lawless One.

Cities were the planting field for the Way of Cain and sin was the plough. In Genesis, God didn't punish cities, he annihilated them. Two cities come immediately to mind today in our nation. They are Las Vegas and New Orleans. They practice voodoo, and dark magic in New Orleans. Las Vegas contains every sort of sensuality and worldliness. Other major cities like New York and Washington D.C. have as dark an imprint but in a different way. All major cities are a magnet for violence and corruption.

10 The Last Descent into the Spirit of Lawlessness

2 Thessalonians 2

For this reason, God sends them a powerful delusion so that they will believe the lie and so that all will be condemned who have not believed the truth but have delighted in wickedness.

The "spirit of lawlessness" will bring in the rule of the Antichrist that will divorce humanity from the truth, except for the very elect of God. The "mystery of iniquity" is secretive and veiled, but intoxicating. It replaces the prevailing Holy Spirit which is removed at the rapture from dominance by this errant seducing spirit. John cited this major characteristic of the Antichrist in his first and second letters. Evidently this was of such importance that it warranted being stated more than once.

In his second letter, John said: "For many deceivers are entered into the world, who confess not that Jesus Christ is come in the flesh. This is a deceiver and an antichrist." The word "anti" in the Greek basically means "counterfeit." The idea that Jesus is just another prophet or teacher strips us of redemption and salvation. The "mystery of iniquity" is putting our hope in ourselves and that life is vain and inclusive. This deception now covers the earth and diminishes the hope in our Savior.

The only thing that separates God's people from the world and the coming judgment is the cross of Christ. Our faith and hope cannot be based on any other foundation. It is why we are to live and it is what is worth dying for. To remove the power of the cross and the divinity of Christ extracts the only hope that we have and leaves us "defenseless" against the radical selfism of the enemy. The next deadly step is replacing Christ with our own selfish perceptions that have the basis of "amoralism" that has its temporary demise. George Barna tells us that eighty-four per cent of those in their twenties claim that the Bible is irrelevant to their profession of moral character.

Morality describes the principled compass that governs our behavior. The Way of Cain destroyed the generation of Noah, because of the moral erosion. The Mystery of Lawlessness is bringing this hellish way of life to fruition at this moment. Abandoning God's moral boundaries brings destruction. Everyone and every nation adhere to a moral doctrine of some kind. We saw the fall of Communism, because of its defective atheistic foundation. The strength or weakness of a free society is the evil as well as the good thrives not from its system but its moral fiber. There are more free societies now than ever before but godlessness is permeating everywhere.

Morality relates on three basic levels. Renowned Christian writer, C.S. Lewis defines these three areas as: to ensure fairness and unity with individuals; to give us a healthy society; and to keep us in a good standing and relationship with God. Based on this definition, it's clear that our beliefs are critical to our moral behavior and yet we are failing in every way. Believing is to "trust in, to cling to and to rely upon God." And if we are honest with ourselves, we see the evidence of this moral collapse all around us every day. As the Way of Cain bled out moral ethic, the Mystery of Lawlessness is causing the fall of the entire planet into the hands of the Antichrist and his imaging. Before, our nation would fall forward learning from our mistakes. We now are freefalling backward with no one to catch us.

Our moral failure since the eclipse of the Sixties is staggering. It began with the failure to embody the ideal of doing the right thing that has its foundation in the Word of God. Just one example of how distorted our thoughts have become is by founder of Planned Parenthood, Margaret Sanger. She once said "the most merciful thing that a family does to one of its infant members is to kill." Western civilization has undergone a dramatic cultural shift. In just a few short years our society has fundamentally altered the meaning of marriage, embraced the notion that men can become women.

There has been moral failure throughout history, especially in godless empires and cities since the Way of Cain. The prophet Isaiah warned, "Woe to those who call evil good and good evil, who put darkness for light and light for darkness, who put bitter for sweet and sweet for bitter. The new normal has taken a more drastic turn called a "moral inversion." This is a sociological phenomenon in which a society's concepts of right and wrong had traded places with each other. This has morally bankrupted every generation in a deeper scale since World War Two. It is apparent in the entire fall on a global scale.

More than four out of five adults contend that they are concerned about the moral condition of the nation. Of the ten moral behaviors evaluated, a majority of Americans believed that each of three activities were "morally acceptable."

Gambling (61%)   Pornography (38%)

Co-Habitation (60%)   Sexual Fantasies (59%)

Abortion (45%)   Adultery (42%).

Pornography (38%)   Drunkenness (35%)

Fornication (56%)   Lying (47%)

A frightening statistic is that 74% of Millennials believe that morality is based on self-perception, not on Biblical truth.

11 The Fruition of Technology in Global Culture

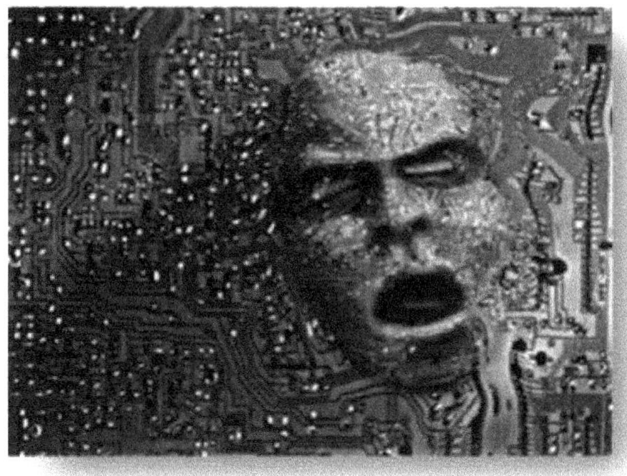

Daniel 12

But you, Daniel, roll up and seal the words of the scroll until the time of the end. Many will go here and there to increase knowledge."

The intervention of the Watchers changed the face of the earth far more than anyone could realize in Noah's day, and it is visiting us again. Cain acquired much of what he needed to erase the burden of the curse through the secret arts of the Watchers. It made their lives far easier and indulgent than known. Even the historic skills of bronze and iron working were not only driven by a desire for ease through plows and tools, but it induced power and warfare through weaponry and other dark adventures.

Today, materialism and technology are rising at an exponential rate. The prophet Daniel warned us that this would lead to the final days of the earth. Our society is unrecognizable, even from a decade ago. Our culture is far more indulgent and separated from God. It is coercing us further from a Biblical mandate and pulling us more and more into the web of the reaper. It is setting up the Mark of the Beast; communications are distorting the relationships between God and man. Technology is not inherently evil, but the course of the age is pulling it more and more into a world devoid of God's will. It is the apparatus that the evil one has encircled the planet with in the last days. The spiritual de-evolution has been mechanized through this spiraling madness. The basis of life has shifted drastically from a Biblical worldview.

Today's globe is shrinking while technology is exploding. The small picture is even more deadly as it is dragging away our young people. Two decades ago, the average child under eighteen spent about fifteen to twenty hours per week digesting media content. Today, it has nearly tripled to almost sixty hours per week of continual time while parents are having children, but not raising them. Young people devote more time to media than to anything other than sleeping. The exposure to media has dropped people's boundaries and restructured their moral code. With substances that are intellectually understood to be potentially harmful, such as gangs, drugs, pornography, alcohol, sexual promiscuity, now bleed through the media. Travel, the internet, television, cell phones and computers put the ends of the earth at our fingertips.

We are even having major revolution in the Middle East inspired through social media. The geometric increase now is changing this generation moment by moment at an unrecognizable proportion. It is prophesied that the advance of robots will reduce the coming job market by over forty per cent. That is a fallen prophecy exposing what the power brokers behind the scene are really after. There is no question that technology has already been a method used to enslave every man, woman and child remaining on the face of the earth through a spiritual worldwide web.

The evolving new monetary system will not only introduce into a Global Cashless Society, but it will use artificial intelligence literally into us in a way that we can't even imagine. There is a global movement to internationalize the banking system as it is moving through the national system. The supposed independence of the Federal Reserve was meant to shield banks from the whims of a president or Congress. Desiring certain policy results. Through the stealth Biden administration, the Federal Reserve is increasingly become a fourth branch of government, especially as politicians try to print their way out of recessions, the pandemic, and excessive government spending. President Biden is continuing inflationary policies, understanding correctly that the balance sheet is double that of the federal budget. Their intent is to take over and nationalize all banks. I shudder how this is progressing, and that every transaction will suffer the over reach of a government that has no financial restriction.

12 The Coming Mark of the Beast

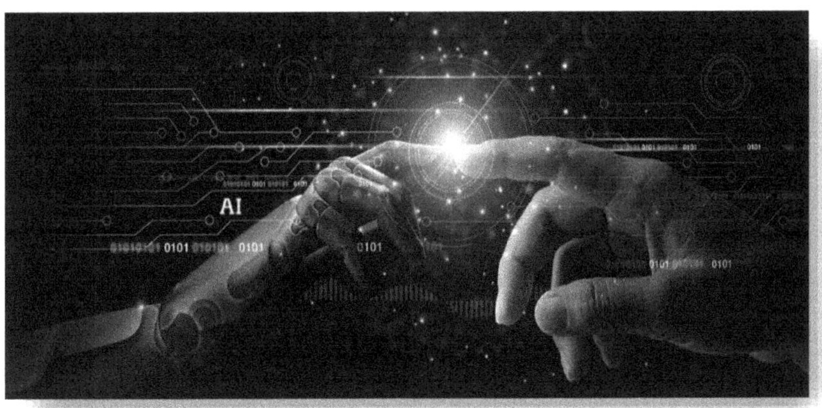

Revelation 13

The second beast was given the power to give breath to the image of the first beast so that the image could speak and cause all who refused to worship the image to be killed.

The greatest blasphemy of Satan is his assault on humanity to steal the image of God. Bringing the image of the Beast to life and enacting it through the Mark of the Beast is the depth of the most narcissistic creature in eternity. Satan's great desire is stealing the worship that only belongs to the Lord. Every hour of this is now relentlessly consuming the masses.

The tapestry of God's Word has opened the infallible truth that humanity will be raped from the image of God to the image of the Beast. This is the carry-over from the Days of Noah. This is in migration and is being implemented through artificial intelligence, nano technology into fatal transhumanism. At this moment, almost eighty per cent of our daily devices and communications feature the rising form of artificial intelligence. This is the coming perfect storm that will ravage the planet as it peeks over the horizon through the eyes of the Beast.

There has never been more concern over the Mark of the Beast than in our present global society. Until the present, neither the technology nor the mindset would have made it possible for this mark to exist. Will there be a mark injected in people's foreheads or their hands to make it possible to buy and sell that will be set up by the Antichrist? This is a very sensitive topic because this technology is exploding all around us, but it is not yet a form of worship. Make no mistake about it, this technology was already placed in the dog in front of me before I got her. I also have a debit card in my wallet that has a chip approved for implant. What the gravest concern for us should be is when they want you chipped to control you into worshipping the Beast because you have been left behind.

With the rise of the RFID technology, we are now on the last leg of the mystery. We can certainly see the possibilities of this becoming a literal reality in our day with the technology of laser beam tattoos, or even under the skin with a hypodermic needle. Now pets are being tracked by tiny computer chips about the size of a grain of rice which have an identification number programmed into it. The most frightening dilemma is the brain chip that has been invented to connect the brain to the computer.

The first thing you need to understand about the Mark of the Beast is that it connects you to the worldwide system that collects and gathers information, and ties it in with personal records of all kinds. This will culminate the implanted chip into your body that will personally connect you to the system. In an instant you will be an enacted slave and worshipper of the Beast. Today you see that information is already being collected when you use your credit or debit card. Many view the Antichrist, the image of the Beast, the Mark of the Beast, and the Beast's alliance to the nations as things that will be easily recognized as evil and sinister. The reality is that the Antichrist will look like the author of this system of government with the greatest and most wonderful religious, political, and economic system the world has ever seen after it has recovered the planet from economic disaster.

We will be looking even deeper and more specific into the return of the Days of Noah and the despicable return of the fallen Watchers. The New World Order is already a shadow government that must eventually have its own currency and control, like the European Union. This issue will provoke and validate the three-pronged attack of global politics, religion, and economics. We are now watching the attacks on constitutional and personal freedoms to break the allegiance to national interest and continuing the regression of the pursuit of holiness and moral fabric for the same reason.

This world and the unbelieving will have the king they have asked for since the days of the prophet Samuel. Wake up church and nation, for while you sleep, the lines are forming. The Antichrist will make it compulsory for everyone to have this tiny microchip implanted under the skin of the right hand or on the forehead. This is to bastardize mankind into the control of the Satan- possessed Antichrist.

12 The Final Global Deception

1 Thessalonians 2

Don't let anyone deceive you in any way, for that day will not come until the rebellion occurs and the man of lawlessness is revealed, the man doomed to destruction. He will oppose and will exalt himself over everything that is called God or is worshiped, so that he sets himself up in God's temple, proclaiming himself to be God.

Empirical government over the centuries began its quest through the primal empires of Egypt and Babylon. These nations were established after the dispersion of Babel and became the seeds for the concurring world empires. The Book of Daniel gives an amazing description on how globalism found its way to the present-day New World Order. Like a spider spinning its web, the evil one has his final apparatus to enslave his victims to enforce his worship.

Globalism has two different meanings and it is different from globalization. The first is the idea of placing the interest of the globe over the individual interest of single nations. Another view is the entire world as a proper sphere for one nation to project political influence. Globalization refers to the culture, people, and economic activities between nations with the fall of national boundaries. It is the life blood of global relationship through control. Both are in tremendous growth and are leading us into a unified globe with the deception of "it's all about me."

There is no question that globalism is eclipsing the earth now. Whether it is military incursion, treaty through the United Nations or environmental implications the earth is now motivated by global initiative. technology and communication, the global society has reached the unity that God solemnly warned us about at the Tower of Babel. It is a paradox of how divided yet how unified we are at the same moment. God warned that nothing would be impossible for mankind under the impact of this toxic umbrella.

The nations are becoming the habitation of the most lethal empire in history. With global communications and the rejection of the truth, the earth is daily being captivated by this lethal idolatrous campaign of the evil one. The global political scene has radically changed since the Second World War. The defeat of Germany and Japan gave rise to the Cold War between the Soviet Union and the West. The Soviet demise and the fall of the Iron Curtain led to the democratization of most of Europe and many other nations. With this change, the thirst for more power and wealth became obsessive in the family of nations.

Cooperation came to the forefront along with a myriad of problems from the reorganization. As the Brave New World Order surfaced, the philosophy from the early global perception that came from as far back as Babel is rising. The idea that man could become one would to accomplish all his dreams. There have always been politicians with this view throughout history. Currently there are countless secret orders and multilateral groups that are feverishly at work.

✥ Chapter Eleven ✥

The Return of the Watchers

Jude 1

And the angels who did not keep their positions of authority but abandoned their proper dwelling—these he has kept in darkness, bound with everlasting chains for judgment on the great Day.

If we could unzip the physical zone, our hearts would stop from envisioning the activity in the spiritual realm today. There is a matrix that is repeating in a geometric advance from the days of the old deluge in today's spirit world. Of all of God's unexpected confrontations Jesus could choose from, why did He use the Days of Noah and Lot as His primary examples? The truth is they were times of total decadence and impending judgment just as we are facing today moment by moment, and they were dispensations of fallen angelic and demonic infestations. This is now demonizing the final global culture as had happened to each kingdom that Daniel prophesied.

As the clock is now tiktoking, we are told in the Book of Matthew that this generation will not pass away until all things are fulfilled. At this point, Christ will have no choice but to remove His remnant church, as He raptured Enoch, before the wickedness of man has come to its complete dissolution in the Great Tribulation. He will remove the true remnant like a thief in the night and He will allow the drastic rebellion to go on unchecked in the Tribulation, before the hand of God crushes the evil world order, that is speedily ripening to its doom.   With sober analysis, I believe there is no question that every detail that defined the generation of Noah is blatant and concluding in our present generation, except for one that has been somewhat veiled in sorcery and technology. This cage is now being opened, slowly releasing the birds of prey from the Days of Noah. The stain of the delusions that swept away Noah's day have become a torrential tsunami deluging the globe from our nation under the wings of these foul birds.

Misconceptions Concerning the Watchers

2 Corinthians 11

And no wonder, for Satan himself masquerades as an angel of light. It is not surprising, then, if his servants also masquerade as servants of righteousness.

In the Jewish Encyclopedia, they chronicled exactly who and what the fallen Watchers were that rebelled. They declared that this evil decadent hybrid race had taught mankind all the arts of deception, witchcraft, and sin without restriction. The main purpose of these delusions was to depersonalize the Lord and his purpose, even to claim that He is just an impersonal energy driving creation. There is a mixture in the Mystery of Lawlessness that appears as a cauldron of powerful delusion stirred into the deceiving lie that God that is just an impersonal energy. The entrance of these deluding masters are even disguised as aliens from other worlds waiting for the right moment. The will induce the coming "great delusion" that the Apostle Paul warned the church in Thessolonica.

At the completion of the Mystery of Lawlessness, God sends this powerful deluding influence as He stops restraining spiritism, granting these deceiving rebels their platform of lies that are portrayed as being above the truth of God's Holy Word. This will sift the inhabitants of the globe that love the profane, and it would deceive the elect of God if it were possible. The Antichrist will then come riding in on his counterfeit white horse to proclaim "peace and safety" as the next horses of the Apocalypse bring the opposite of peace with war, pandemic, and death. This begins the first part of the Tribulation where man reaps what he has sown, getting the false king they always wanted. Satan will become this hybrid king masquerading as the light.

The Returning Caged Birds of the Days of Noah

Revelation 18

And he shouted with a mighty voice, saying, "Fallen, fallen is Babylon the great! She has become a dwelling place for demons, a dungeon haunted by every unclean spirit, and a prison for every unclean and loathsome bird. For all the nations have drunk from the wine of the passion of her sexual immorality, and the kings and political leaders of the earth have committed immorality with her, and the merchants of the earth have become rich by the wealth and economic power of her sensuous luxury."

Could it be that we are looking with our eyes, and not enlivened spirits? We know that the Days of Noah were not to be unique, because of the presence of the fallen Watchers and their hybrid offspring. The parable of the Mustard Tree given by Jesus is the shortest and most misunderstood parable in the scripture. It reveals what happens to the kingdom of God in its expansion into an abnormal huge tree. Ironically, at the end of the church age, there are demonic foul birds that lodge in its branches. These are the same birds that are caged in the Book of Revelation to be released by the mysterious Harlot of Babylon who rides the global Beast. This truth is this parable is one of the most misunderstood and profound exposes the spiritual return of the fallen Watchers from the Days of Noah. They have returned to extend the Way of Cain through the present Mystery of Lawlessness as they nestled in women during the Days of Noah.

The history of the fallen Watchers is oblivious to most and a distortion to many. During the hideous entry through the era of the "Sixties," they ferociously infested a recurring rancid rebellion of drugs, sensuality, sorcery, and unbelief from Noah's day to the ends of the earth. There is no question that they are the fallen angels that entered from the Garden of Eden and they will have their part in consummating the devastating delusion at the end of the Tribulation.

Their last final assault will be at the end of the Tribulation when these specific rapists are released from "Tartarus," the abyss by the "Destroyer" to torment the people who do not have the seal of God on their foreheads. They are not permitted to kill anyone, but to torment and cause them extreme pain for five months. There is no doubt that there will be the release of these spiritual renegades to inflict their horrific imprint in the final hour.

Yet, what present activities are taking place that is seductively hidden from our eyes? Satan and his cohorts relish in disguise and operate within a veil of secrecy. Most today believe that the current influence of fallen angels appears to be mainly operating through just dark spiritual influences, but they are captivating the hearts and minds of the unbelieving with oppression by the system of the world order. There is a countless collage of spiritual interventions that cloud the media and the internet.

Myriads of conspiracy theories are on the web that confuse and camouflage the reality of what is truly taking place. The fascination from hybrid reptilians to alien beings confuse the issue of the fallen Watchers to disguise their future ascent from the abyss while the others are at work in the final hour. We must be soberly discerning about what is true and not be deluded by the things that are masked through the "Great Delusion." Spiritism, occultism, political, and fleshly ways have led to this full rebellion. Seduction and sensuality have opened the gates of astrology, UFOs, aliens, magic, Wicca, and New Age perversion to bring to bear these evil spirits that have captivated this mirrored age of deception that would even deceive the elect if it were possible..

There is now suspect extra-Biblical input that gives credit to beings from another cosmos that are foreign to God's creation. There also is a growing phenomenon within the scientific and psychological field of bizarre reports from those that claim to have been abducted by the inhabitants of alien spacecraft. There is some speculation that this replicates the lawless acts of the Watchers from the generation of Noah. These reports seem too bizarre to accept, yet too often confessed but too consistent to ignore. It is imperative that we stay within the boundaries and integrity of scripture, but not be ignorant or refuse the testimonies that are valid and verified.

Satan has provoked many avenues to camouflage his corrupt intention through the ages including deception in the heavens. For the most part, these invasive creatures are veiled or redefined as aliens or other spiritual guides today, because the Prince of this World hates to be exposed by the Light. The obsession with extraterrestrials has entered this arena and has caused great confusion and a disguise for these fallen watchers to be misdiagnosed as intergalactic beings instead of inter-dimensional beings that operate in the spiritual realm. Dr. John Mack, a professor of psychiatry at Harvard Medical School, and a former Pulitzer Prize winner, has been involved in almost a hundred cases, and testified that these beings may be real and that they appear to have an agenda to develop a hybrid race.

The Deceptive Extraterrestrials and the UFO Phenomena

2 Thessalonians 2

Don't let anyone deceive you in any way, for that day will not come until the rebellion occurs and the man of lawlessness is revealed, the man doomed to destruction.

It is inevitable that these inhabiting spirits from hell will introduce extra-terrestrial deception to cover their tracks. Right now, it is mysterious why our government has held back all the research and sightings on extraterrestrials. There has been an overwhelming body of evidence for the apparent visitation of these beings to earth, including literally tens of thousands of eyewitness accounts which they claim should be enough to convince any skeptic that we are not alone in the universe. But are they really aliens or a great deception?

No one ever seems quite sure what they really saw, but the sightings are usually striking. This is part of the growing fascination with the possibility of intelligent alien life. The belief in UFOs and extraterrestrials is becoming a type of obsession, and it isn't nearly as fringe as you might think. Over sixty percent of young Americans believe in intelligent extraterrestrial life. This tracks closely with the belief in God but is that just an accident? The appeal of this belief says volumes about our culture and the shifting roles of religion and technology. It's really a deep look at how myths and religions were created in the beginning, and how human beings deal with the unknown.

In the twenty-first century, the belief of life in outer space is taken for granted by our educational and media establishments, and with this assumption comes the inevitable discussion of UFOs and alien life forms. The Great Delusion from the Mystery of Lawlessness will surely include the fallen Watchers returning being masqueraded as aliens from the heavens. There are myriads of people that innocently believe in what they have even seen but when it comes down to it, what have they truly seen?

One of the most striking innovations within contemporary spiritualism is the adoption of extraterrestrials as spirit guides by some contemporary spiritualists. It is here that the New Age fascination with extraterrestrials and UFOs has taken on a uniquely spiritual form. Extraterrestrials have come to represent for many spiritualists the successful achievement of the goal: the union between spirituality and science.

The Secret Government Endeavors

There are countless conspiracy theories about government cover ups spanning from the beginning of our nation concerning things from the Masonic Order to the secret and occultic leaven from the deep state and godless politicians with hellish intentions. We will focus on just a few of these that are relevant in this hour. For decades, stories of alien abductions, UFO encounters, flying saucer sightings, and Area 51 have led millions of people to believe that extraterrestrials are secretly among us. But what if those millions of people are all wrong? What if the UFO phenomenon has a much darker and far more sinister history from the Days of Noah?

For years, UFO specialists have been investigating the mysterious world of a secret group within the U.S. Government known as the Collins Elite. This group believes that our purported alien visitors are, in reality, deceptive demons and fallen angels. They are the fallen Watchers of Satan, who are reaping and enslaving our very souls, and paving the way for the Valley of Decision and Judgment Day. There are secret government files on occultists Aleister Crowley and Jack Parsons that are mentioned later about their connections to the UFO mystery; revelations of the demonic link to the famous "UFO crash" at Roswell, New Mexico. Also, the disclosure of government investigations into life-after-death and out-of-body experiences; and an examination of the satanic agenda behind alien abductions. Final Events reveals the stark and horrific truths about UFOs that some in the government would rather keep secret.

In June 1978, a French government UFO study group concluded that "with everything taken into consideration, a material phenomenon seems to be behind the totality of flying machines whose modes of sustenance, and propulsion are beyond our knowledge. If the UFO mystery is indeed beyond the grasp of our understanding is there more reason to strive towards learning more about it?

Our government has been far less open and has always been stonewalling what has been really going on. Newly declassified documents from the Pentagon, reveal they have funded projects that investigated UFOs, wormholes, alternate dimensions, and a host of other subjects that are deeply related to the Watcher deception or to aliens. It will evidently be veiled until it is shouted from the rooftops. There seems to be a growing concern within the psychiatric community from the strange reports from people who claim to have been "abducted" by the occupants of UFOs. These reports are too bizarre to accept, and yet too frequent to ignore. The U.S. government's interest in UFOs is neither shocking, nor revelatory.

These only further confirmed what countless investigations that are only to defer the truth. The pathway to understanding these mysterious government programs will take you through the catacombs of secret societies, through the military, aerospace, and the intelligence communities. UFOs have been receiving newfound levels of government scrutiny not seen in decades. Congress has expressed concern that America's airspace is not as safe as we think.

In this era of unparalleled technological advances, as Artificial Intelligence reshapes our world order, believers are faced with many deafening questions: Is there a trace of AI in Biblical prophecy? Will the Antichrist manipulate this technology to proclaim godhood through this avenue? Asking these same questions, prophecies and the unfolding of global events will truly expose the devil as the author of confusion who seeks to make us doubt God's sovereignty.

The Abyss Called Tartarus

Revelation 9

They had as king over them the angel of the Abyss, whose name in Hebrew is Abaddon and in Greek is Apollyon (that is, Destroyer).

The term, "Dudael" is implied to be the prison of all the fallen angels, which is the entrance located to the east of Jerusalem. The way this place is described is sometimes considered as a region of the underworld, comparable to Tartarus. The ancient Greeks believed that the earth was hollow and that inside of this planet was a realm where other 'beings' were kept imprisoned. This interior of the earth the Greeks named Tartarus. It is the deep abyss that is used as a dungeon of torment and is generally understood to be the place where the hundreds of fallen Watchers are imprisoned.

Tartarus is described as the place where "the Watchers" are mentioned in the context of what Jesus did in the time between His death and resurrection. After being made alive, he went and made proclamation to the imprisoned spirits, to those who were disobedient long ago when God waited patiently in the Days of Noah, while the ark was being built. This fascinating topic has given way to speculation on how these Watchers are eventually released by Apollyon in the Great Tribulation. We need to be careful in this prophetic endeavor not to speculate past the evidence of the scripture.

There are so many deceptive opinions in social media and the internet, already that cause great confusion. As the seeds of technology is now mushrooming advances that would even curl Albert Einstein's hair. The canvas of tools allowing Noah to build the ark to the pyramids, expose mechanical reveal the hidden knowledge of what occurred in the Days of Noah. Our exponential growth of technology is immeasurable. The smartphone alone in your pocket provides a better communication tool than the President of the United States had access to just two decades ago, and provides access to more data than he had access to just ten years ago.

As we covered before, the fallen Watchers opened a Pandora's Box of secret magical arts and knowledge that were flooded during the Great Deluge. If not for the saving grace of God, this planet would have ripened its doom long before now. We will see in eternity the full depth of the eternal salvation of humanity that occurred at the flood and soon with this generation. We are warned that the Antichrist and the False Prophet will produce unimaginable lying wonders as we are pulled from the coming economic morass. We are already witnessing geometrical explosions of technology that certainly are being provoked by the returned fallen Watchers in their hidden nests before they are exposed.

The Opening Portal to the Abyss

Job 38

Have the gates of death been revealed to you? Or have you seen the doors of deep darkness?

There is a banishing ritual in witchcraft where a cauldron is filled that imitates a black hole. They say that if you throw something into the cauldron, you can watch it disappear into the cosmic abyss. The Rite of Manifestation also allows participants standing in the circle of the pentagram when it is cast to pass through spirit portals for a limited duration. Spirit portals are created in the spirit world as doorways into the physical world from the spiritual or vice versa.

It has suspected that there will be created portals or gateways to bring the Watchers back from the abyss that they were imprisoned in at the flood. The spiritual realities can often be more bizarre than fantasy. There are so many speculations on how this will occur. This will be one of the lying wonders that will occur during the Great Tribulation and then surface completely. In 1918, occultist Aleister Crowley, who we spoke of earlier attempted to create a dimensional vortex that would bridge the gap between the world of the visible and the spiritual realm. He called it the "Amalantrah Working" and according to Crowley it was successful when a presence manifested itself through the portal.

Thirty years later, the "Amalantrah Working" was attempted to be recreated by rocket scientist, Jack Parsons, one of the founders of NASA and his cohort L. Ron Hubbard from the Church of Scientology. They tried again with second ritual called, "Babylon Working." They attempted to reopen the gateway that was originally tried by Crowley. They wanted to portal into the spirit of Babylon, and to invoke the spirit of the Mysterious Harlot of Babylon to the planet. Again, the core of this process was part of the secret knowledge recreated from the Days of Noah. It cannot be proven, but the claim is that the Enochian magic from the Watchers had succeeded and that the Harlot of Babylon is hovering the earth today. Even conservative evangelical ufologists draw on secular ufologists such as Jacques Vallée who argued that UFOs could not be from outer space and must be interdimensional. The marriage of the spiritual and technology is creating a paradigm of deep deception erasing God from the mind of the masses into another abyss of sorcery.

The Mystical Hadron Collider by CERN

Job 38

Have the gates of death been revealed to you? Or have you seen the doors of deep darkness?

A portal is defined as a large and imposing gate or doorway into a castle, a cathedral, or even on an internet site. Portals can be used to describe other types of doorways, both literal, inter-dimensional and spiritual. The term "portal" has saturated this generation through social media, and a plethora of video games to normalize its use. The Social Media Portal is a news and information directory mapping all aspects of social media globally. This has become a "yellow brick road" of the mind leading to lawlessness. Next, we will peer into what technology is doing with it.

There is an amazing project that on its surface is just a scientific experiment, but when you look deeper it already had chilling effects in the spiritual realm. It is a global achievement with boundless possibilities. We shouldn't be surprised to see things like this surfacing. In Sweden, there is a group called CERN that has spent billions on the Hadron Collider which is a massive bizarre machine that is supposedly to be a particle smasher in the name of quantum physics. Scientists claim the Large Hadron Collider, is a way to explore science and the mystery to the glue that holds together the particles of the universe.

It has been discovered that they are crossing over into the spiritual realm for transference. Mankind has always looked for a gateway or a stairway to heavenly ascension since the Tower of Babel. This project is an atomic marvel that has destructible qualities and the intention of being a gateway for some very mystical reasons. It was reopened this year after retooling with twice the power in magnification. Over the years, CERN has always claimed to be open to the scientific communities of all nations, overcoming political barriers. CERN scientists worked with their Soviet and US counterparts throughout the Cold War. It is no accident that many Eastern European countries joined CERN soon after the fall of the Berlin Wall. And today, scientists from all regions of the world gather at the laboratory.

The Mysterious CERN Gateway

In March of 1989, Tim Berners-Lee, a scientific engineer at CERN, had submitted a proposal to develop a radically new way of linking and sharing of information on an internet shoulder. This began the authorization of the World Wide Web is the gate that birthed and opened through international communication. How mystifying that this technical marvel has the name that it has as it completes its mission to bring the final assault of the Watchers from the abyss.

The next step in this bizarre process is very bewildering and it is very strange. This particle collider is the largest machine in the world. It took thousands of scientists, engineers and technician's decades to plan and build, and it continues to operate at the very boundaries of scientific knowledge.

The Hadron Collider will not generate black holes in the cosmological sense. However, some theories suggest that the formation of tiny 'quantum' black holes in the dark matter of the universe may be a very distinct possibility. Mankind has looked for a gateway or stairs to heavenly ascension.

CERN has had a primary goal to validate and prove the existence of what is called "the Higgs field." It would be a monumental discovery for science and human knowledge, and would open doorways to new knowledge in many so-called disciplines. The simplest means to test the existence of the Higgs field would be a search for a new elementary particle that the field would have to give off, a particle known as "Higgs bosons" or the "God particle". Since the sixties, scientists have been studying the existence of what is called "the Higgs Field." To clarify, the Higgs field has been proposed as the energy of the vacuum, which supposedly is about the extreme energies of the first moments of the "Big Bang." caused the universe to be a kind of featureless symmetry of integrated extremely high energy.

There is great speculation of the dangers and motives of this complicated and mysterious machine and its process. There is even concern that this could cause a reaction that could literally destroy the universe. At the least it appears that we are becoming "the Sorcerer's New Apprentice" that could open the doors or gateways that were never meant to be opened.

This takes the intent of a universal evolution into a deeper darker doorway. It claims it is a grandiose undertaking to shed light on the esoteric world of particle physics, but also on international collaboration, purpose, and progress. There is a fine line between the physical laws and the spiritual ones. It is extremely difficult to discern the motives that thrive in scientific attempts truly having spiritual means and intents. Now, China is in the process of standing on the shoulders of this project with the same intent.

The spiritual dynamic thread through all of this is bewildering and evident. Why is a hideous Hindu god perched as the main piece on the CERN campus? What are the underlying spiritual aspects hidden in its symbolism? For those not steeped in Eastern spirituality, the Lord Shiva is one of the three primary deities of the Hindu trinity, and is known wherever his image is worshiped as the destroyer and transformer. The main icons of Shiva are the third eye on his forehead, which is also on the back of our dollar bill, the serpent Vasuki around his neck, the adorning crescent moon, the holy river Ganga flowing from his matted hair, the trisula as his weapon and the "damaru" as his musical instrument.

There is a mysterious web of hidden vultures that have sold their souls in secrecy in this final hour for this intent. This has profound implications of the fallen Watchers input and their spiritual impact. Around Shiva is a gateway of fire that it dances in the middle of. It is also compelling that this demon is portrayed as genderless. What does this dancing Shiva have to do with the Large Hadron Collider? This cosmic dancer performs his divine dance to destroy a weary universe and prepare for God Brahma to start the new process of creation. Shiva is coming through a gateway of fire.

As we covered in the Book of Revelation, the abyss is opened releasing the imprisoned spirits of the fallen Watchers during the close of the Great Tribulation. Then Satan and his rebels are cast to the earth through supernatural action. The Greek defines the king, a fallen angelic messenger, has keys to open the Abyss. This angel's name is Abaddon or Apollyon, which means the Destroyer, which matches the exact description of Shiva, the Hindu destroyer perched in the gate of CERN.

In 1995, even the gnostic, Carl Sagan wrote a book, "The Demon-Haunted world: Science as a candle in the dark." He focused on distinguishing science from pseudoscience, specifically on witchcraft, UFOs, ESP, and faith healing. The book illustrates Sagan's commitment to base life on the importance of rigorous questioning of ideas furthered from the Age of Reason. As Sagan marked up his draft with a considerable number of cross outs, rewrites and additions, it exposed his own trap of "ever learning but never coming to the knowledge of the truth.". There are so many prophecies and warnings that the Lord has bestowed on us so that we would not be caught unaware as they were in the generation of Noah. That is why we are compelled to be wise as a serpent but harmless as a dove. Technology has catapulted us into a culture traveling at the speed of light. We are experiencing a global chess game where the pieces continue to migrate, because humanity continues to base life on the Great Lie from Eden and the serpent, that we are gods and He is not.

The Fruition of the Watcher's Deadly Technology

Daniel 12

Those who are wise will shine like the brightness of the heavens, and those who lead many to righteousness, like the stars for ever and ever. But you, Daniel, roll up and seal the words of the scroll until the time of the end. Many will go here and there to increase knowledge."

When we look back at the impact of the first Industrial Revolution, the changes are staggering in technology and culture. The world wars then birthed another wave of technology to drastically change these two issues even further. As the family dinner went from the dinner table with conversation to TV trays and TV dinners, we begin to fade into the technology of media. The movie theater, the music scene and a myriad of sorcerous idols produced an ever-imploding black hole as our moral fabric begin to dissolve.

Space flight then took us into a techno-explosion of immense proportion. The cellphone, the computer and social media kidnapped our kids, as our Lord was dismissed from the family as He was from our government and our schools. Even more sobering is these screens are now beginning to stare through these electronic devices while we stare back at them. Husbands and their sons hide making love to the daughters of men through a screen as it destroys relationships and family.

As we are returning to the decadence of the Days of Noah and Sodom, they are returning to us. We have little comprehension the idolatrous utensils of sorcery like cities, weapons, music, witchcraft, and government that were the seeds that were sown that we now stand in the field that was planted. The Watchers have returned behind the veil while they continue their seduction in living techno-color.

Tragically, we have opened the Pandora's Box that will not be shut. The final missing piece is arriving as a wolf in sheep's clothing. The extension of science with artificial intelligence will be the returning sin of the Watchers that seductively raped women in Genesis, creating hybrid Nephilim. This is the point where it will not be hybrid offspring but the artificial intelligence hybridizing humanity into the computer. Artificial intelligence is morphing by the minute as we truly are entering the Brave New World we were warned would come.

The five industrial revolutions are coal, gas, electronics and nuclear technology, the internet and a renewable energy era, and the present artificial intelligence era. Beginning from eighteenth century through the present day, we've seen an amazing evolution in technology impact culture. As we discovered different energy sources and later, digital technologies, the entire landscape of the modern world has transformed over and over.

Here's a brief primer on the five industrial revolutions

First Industrial Revolution: the Coal Era:

The original Industrial Revolution transformed our economy from agriculture to industry. Processes became mechanized, and products were manufactured for the first time. During this period, the discovery of coal and its mass extraction, as well as the development of the steam engine and metal forging, completely changed the way goods were produced and exchanged. Inventions such as spinning loom to make fabric were making their appearance.

Second Industrial Revolution: the Gas Era:

As the first industrial revolution was driven by coal, the second revolved around the discovery of electricity, gas and oil. The invention of the combustion engine went hand-in-hand with these fuel sources. Both steels, and chemically based products like plastic entered the market during this time. Developments in communication technology got a jump start with the telegraph and later the telephone. Transportation grew by leaps and bounds with the invention of the plane and car. Mechanical production grew in speed through the advent of mass production.

Third Industrial Revolution: the Electronic and Nuclear Era:

After another hundred years, nuclear energy and electronics enter the landscape. Nuclear power began in Europe, grew in both Great Britain and the United States, went into remission for years, and grew in Asia. This continued the alienation of humanity from their Creator.

Fourth Industrial Revolution: Internet and Renewable Energy Era:

As we continue moving through the fourth industrial revolution, we see a shift to renewable energy such as solar, wind and geothermal under the guise and fear of climate change. However, the momentum comes not from the shift in energy but from the acceleration of digital technology. The internet and the digital world mean a real-time connection within more and more components of a production line, both inside and outside facility walls. As the development of the Industrial Internet of Things, cloud technology and artificial intelligence continue, a virtual world will merge with the physical world. Predictive maintenance and real-time data will lead to smarter business decisions for a myriad of companies around the world.

Fifth Industrial Revolution: the Final Artificial Intelligence Era:

In simple terms, robots are being made to mock human behavior illustrating artificial intelligence. According to the Oxford dictionary, AI is demonstrated by machines that have cerebral agents to perceive the outer environment to make logical decisions and maximize the success of a task. In brief, to be their own gods from their creator. Does that sound familiar? AI is the technology of the future generation that is beginning to revolutionize the entire world. We are already living it. Smart products, smart homes, speech assistants (the Alexa you love to hear) were born from AI. There is no doubt that technology is evolving at the speed of light, but I believe artificial intelligence is yet to evolve in its supreme form, as the new Nephilim of the final hour becoming a hybrid linked to DNA.

Stephen Hawking said, "success in creating effective AI, could be the greatest or the worst event in the history of our civilization. We just don't know. So, we cannot know if we will be infinitely helped by AI, or ignored by it and side-lined, or conceivably destroyed by it." The main motto of artificial intelligence is to create intelligent machines that can perform tasks that typically require human intelligence. Our era is being driven by the final Industrial Revolution.

The prophet Daniel said, "there would be only one "time of trouble, for Israel such as never was since there was a nation even to that same time." As we witness the perpetual technical war in the Middle East, the web of the evil of the rising "Fourth Reich is with lying wonders.

The Lie About Witnessing Extraterrestrals

Jude 1

And the angels who did not stay within their own position of authority, but left their proper dwelling, he has kept in eternal chains under gloomy darkness until the judgment of the great day.

After being cast from heaven, these renegades know their eternal fate would eventually be the lake of fire, so they feel they have nothing to lose if they don't find a new habitation or a dwelling place both personal and as a regime. After banishment to the second heaven, they sought a place and in what better of a place than God's new creature in his image and their domain. Since their premier assault on earth during the Days of Noah, these monsters have wreaked havoc and desecrated the planet.

For a long time, extraterrestrials have been perceived as highly superior to us because their science appears to exceed our own by myth. Few understand the false authors of higher order came in the Days of Noah with their own techno-explosion that was verified from the ark to the pyramids. The adoption of aliens as spirit guides can be seen both as a 'rationalization' of spiritual belief through a strong idealization of science, and the opportunity to inject this lying philosophy into the spiritual realm.

The Dark Ages came to fruition from the decay of the Roman empire that brought in tumultuous times by brutal invaders. As daily life in the Dark Ages was dictated by wealth, power, status and a feudal system, the invading watchers sit in the nest of their delusion feeding the masses. The sifting of tribalistic unions are hastening the return to a final new dark age seeded in the closing of the Days of Noah. As the Bible has been locked up again, the lost in in the dark are enslaved by the systematized Roman return, creating a black hole of spiritual despair.

Because these watchers know of their eternal fate, they try to drag down as many souls as possible with them in hope of conquering God's image. Their weapons of temptation, seduction, demonic oppression and possession, have returned in the full force of rebellion that will end by the Messiah in the Valley of Decision.

The Fruition of the Watcher's Deadly Sorcery

2 Thessalonian 2

Don't let anyone deceive you in any way, for that day will not come until the rebellion occurs and the man of lawlessness[1] is revealed, the man doomed to destruction. He will oppose and will exalt himself over everything that is called God or is worshiped, so that he sets himself up in God's temple, proclaiming himself to be God.

The Way of Cain and the fallen Watchers have again unleashed the fermenting lie with the Mystery of Lawlessness. It is mesmerizing to realize that the hidden message of the "Great Lie" is also breeding from the Satanic bible and the occult message of the third eye as the heart of the New Age and New World Order. They are a mirror of one another and one in the same. Most people do not understand that Satanism is not centered on worshipping Satan, but it is focused on worshipping "self."

The Satanist spouts, "do what you will" as the New Ager quotes, "create your own reality." There is nothing "new" about it and there is no difference in truth. These are both the same mantra from the hellish fall of Adam and Eve. It strips you from any acknowledgement or submission to the will of God. It excludes the Holy Spirit and it inspires the self-centered delusion that 'we are gods" evolving into a prison of arrogant delusion.

It is the subtle, hidden and deadly toxin that has fermented from the beginning and filling the cup of the final Harlot of Babylon. It is impossible to minimize the deadly potion that existed before the origin of the gospel and the early church. This potion has permeated every level of our global society and is coming to a final fruition. It has traveled as a disease all the way from Eden to the halls of our Congress and is leavened in the nominal church through the seed of apostasy. It has tragically leaved the whole lump as it did in the days of Noah.

◈ Chapter Twelve ◈

Learning from the Days of Noah

2 Peter 2

For if God did not spare angels when they sinned, but sent them to hell, putting them in chains of darkness to be held for judgment; if he did not spare the ancient world when he brought the flood on its ungodly people, but protected Noah, a preacher of righteousness, and seven others.

The return of Jesus Christ will be the pinnacle of human history. The current birth pains of His return will be your greatest mercy or your gravest travesty as the Great Tribulation comes to your door; when your fate will be sealed. It will proceed from mankind's darkest hour, where the unrighteousness will have run their course to the eternal sifting of planet earth. As in Noah's day, it will bring a severe reminder of the betrayal that God so deeply felt that He repented that He had ever made them, as the guilty refused to repent. The four horsemen of the apocalypse will pierce the horizon with their final assault, as the remnant prepare to escape into the arms of their Redeemer at His beckoned call.

The provocation of the Great Deluge not only came with the invasion of the fallen Watchers, but it was even more about the unrepentant hearts of the men of Noah's day that deferred their allegiance to the Prince of Darkness. Without God as the anchor of their souls, their hearts went dark as they drifted into the abyss of "selfism," with no vision or hope. In the above scriptures, the Apostle Peter emphasized the judgement of the fallen angels would be held back to give room for repentance of Noah's generation.

As Noah labored for over a hundred years, the Lord wept over the children of disobedience that took the Way of Cain, thinking they were the center of the universe. They crafted their sin under the invading master of doom and his imps. Later, these angelic traitors were imprisoned in chains in the heart of the earth. They have waited there for their release of vengeance upon the final rebels at the end of the Great Tribulation. As with the perversion of the generation of Noah reached its final decay, the ark of salvation was finished by Noah and his family, and the unthinkable finally came and baptized the earth. Not one other soul had repented of their disobedience or unbelief. The hour of judgment is returning upon this generation as the faithful remnant will finally be swept awayinto the sky. The sobering revelation of the remnant from Noah is speaking today to the nominal church of whom will be left behind.

The Closing Door

Genesis 7

The animals going in were male and female of every living thing, as God had commanded Noah. Then the Lord shut him in.

Matthew 25

"But while they were on their way to buy the oil, the bridegroom arrived. The virgins who were ready went in with him to the wedding banquet. And the door was shut.

One of God's specific instructions for Noah was to build a massive door in the side of the ark. Noah and his family entered this same door to be saved from the flood when the Lord had to shut the door. As the flood ensued, Noah surely heard the fervent pleas outside to open the massive door, but the truth is, only the Lord could have opened it. It was the partition between the unbelieving outside of the door and those that worked out their salvation with fear and trembling.

The New Testament account of the door closing is the parable of the Ten Virgins. In this parable, virgins went forth to meet the bridegroom with their lamps. Five were wise in that they took extra oil for their lamps and five were foolish, because though they took their lamps, they did not take extra oil. When the Bridegroom finally came, the foolish virgins found that their lamps had gone out, and they had to go get more oil in the outer darkness. While they were out to buy their oil, the bridegroom came. They that were ready went in with him to the marriage celebration as the door was shut. Afterward came the other virgins, saying Lord, Lord, open to us. But he answered and said, "Truly, I say to you, I never knew you."

Obviously, the grand lesson of these two accounts is that one must be prepared, and full of wisdom when the time comes. There are serious things to be aware of when God shuts the door. First, is when God shuts the door, it reveals His patience has run out. Throughout all of the ages, God demonstrated His patience and longsuffering with sinful man, and He continues to do so today. But, as the time came for the flood, the time will come when God's patience has come to an end in the Day of Evil. The anger of the Lord is always tied to the end of His patience. His feelings are also tied by His righteous indignation.

There has been a continual dispute among the nominal church about whether a Christian can lose their salvation. even though it is not possible, because salvation is a gift from God, not to be revoked. This is a matter between the temporal and eternity. Sadly, many today use this for a license for apathy and sin, disgracing the cross. This is exactly why the Apostle Paul warned the childlike church in Corinth to be careful what they are building, because you can be saved by fire with your earthly being burned up. There is a bigger picture than just personal concern. This is what has brought us here.

This is also why Paul warned in the Book of Hebrews, "Today, if you will hear His voice, do not harden your hearts." Unfortunately, there is a general lack of the fear of the Lord in the body of Christ today, and even an anger to say, "just leave me alone!" This part has come through reckless pillows today saying a believer can say and live any way they want because their past, present, and future sins have already been forgiven. This is the apostasy we were warned would return that is in part ; the great rebellion that is synonymous with the days of Noah. We need a sense of urgency as He returns as a thief in the night to snatch away the remnant of jewels at the twinkling of an eye. It will be the most sobering time in history for the apathetic and apostate. We must purchase the oil for our lamps as we wait for our Bridegroom with patient endurance.

The Continuing Sins of the Fathers

Numbers 14

The Lord is slow to anger and abundant in lovingkindness, forgiving iniquity and transgression; but He will by no means clear the guilty, visiting the iniquity of the fathers on the children to the third and the fourth generations.'

The tattoo on the back of this young woman from her social page, represents the cry from today's Generation Z that is a reprint from the Days of Noah. This is a testament of what lies at their door, as they are gripping every tangible. As the Apostle Paul warned with tears "many live as enemies of the cross of Christ. Their destiny is destruction, their god is their senses, and their glory is in their shame. Life without God truly leaves you with no love, no hope, and no true reason for living."

The Book of Ecclesiastes compels us that life is fleeting at best without responding to eternity "being set in the heart of man." This generation is looming like a blind man that dwells in his own house, feeling his way through the corridors of familiarity. Without the will of God in our lives, we are left at the peril of this world and its devices going through the motions of hiding in the selfish desires of false fulfilment. As the young lady, testified on her back in the image, "Where is my love? Where is my hope? Where is my reason for living? This is an outcry of our young kids concerning their purpose and destiny in the day of testing that has come upon us.

As I spent nearly three decades ministering to young people in the juvenile justice system in Colorado, I watched the landslide of amorality, spiritual deficit, and unbelief create a black hole in the hearts and souls of a desperate generation, captured in the same corruptive cauldron of Noah, deeply at work in their prodigal culture. Our post Christian society has become in a large extent a profane witness that has gradually married the values and culture that are not what we were founded upon. It is undeniable that we have lost our way as a nation, a culture and a nuclear family. We have slowly become the reflection of Noah's culture that had divorced God, leaving Him heart-broken again. We have continued the Way of Cain and have visited it upon our children. We will be sifted to follow the Way of Cain, or the way of Noah.

The Deadly Sin of Unbelief

Hebrews 3

See to it, brothers, and sisters, that none of you has a sinful, unbelieving heart that turns away from the living God. See to it, brothers, and sisters, that none of you has a sinful, unbelieving heart that turns away from the living God. But encourage one another daily, if it is called "Today," so that none of you may be hardened by sin's deceitfulness.

The sin of unrepentance ushered in unbelief through the door in the Days of Noah. It was not that Cain denied the existence of God, for he was well familiar with Him. God had spoken to him and had invested in him. He was supposed to be the one carrying the mantle of redemption for the race as the firstborn of Adam and Eve. God even confronted him to repent and believe as his brother, Abel, but he chose another father in Lucifer, and began to build upon the unbelief of his fallen parents. Unbelief is based in rejecting and rebelling against God, not the denial of His existence.

Even today the greatest issue is not the belief that God doesn't exist. Eighty per cent in our nation claim to acknowledge the existence of God. The tragic truth is that God has become a legend in their own mind. It is about refusing to repent from a selfish perspective and to receive a personal accountability to him. Any religious philosophy that excludes this is inherited from the deadliest of the sin on the earth.

Unbelief and unrepentance are the twin sins from the Days of Noah. To understand what is truly defined as unbelief, we must first realize what belief truly is. Belief is truly embracing Jesus for who He truly is, seeing him as the eternally valued Son of God, following Him as Lord and Savior through believing. Our faith is active when know that God exists as we trust in Him, rely on Him and cling to Him. It is not just acknowledging the fact that he is the Son of God, but also seeing him as infinitely the precious way, the truth, and the life. The fallen angels and demons knew who He was, but they did not trust in Him, and in turn, rejected him.

It is important to understand the word "unbelief" represents two Greek words, "apothecia" meaning "disobedience" and "apistia" meaning "distrust." Apostasy is rooted in this word which is the antithesis of faith. This defines the two basic issues of unbelief; disobeying God and not putting your trust in Him. This perfectly describes the heart in "the Way of Cain." Cain had no interest in God's way or His approval. His heart was frozen and so was his love for others. This also describes the present generation in its defiance in precept and even more in disobedience. The cancer of narcissism has spread violently and quenched the validity of faith and relationship in this generation.

There were two spirits that marveled Jesus that are sifting humanity. One was the spirit of unbelief, and the other was the spirit of faith. These two opposing spirits have operated in the lives of all human beings. Until you decide and make up in your mind that you are going to believe the Word of God, regardless of circumstances or situations, then you will always be wavering between these two spirits. There are carnal Christians who have made the decision to be saved by forgiveness, have gotten the guarantee of Heaven, and then live a life of total disobedience by putting themselves still on the throne.

Eternal vision has no value to the unbelieving and the unrepentant, but temporal blessing is everything. In Proverb 28, the wise King Solomon declared, "Where there is no vision, the people perish." As in many places in the Bible, the "stiff necked" is used as a figure of speech to speak to the stubborn attitude that resists and turns to look away. This proverb speaks about the man who is often rebuked but doesn't listen to the rebuke; instead, he stiffens his neck." A stiff neck gives you no way to see what is going on around you. They no longer have a standard greater than their own feelings or current opinions. This has become the "new normal." How tragic to stand before Christ at his judgment and He responds, "what do you want from Me? You have already received your reward on earth.

The Deadly Sin of Unrepentance

Hebrews 6

It is impossible for those who have once been enlightened, who have tasted the heavenly gift, who have shared in the Holy Spirit, who have tasted the goodness of the word of God and the powers of the coming age and who have fallen away, to be brought back to repentance. To their loss they are crucifying the Son of God all over again and subjecting him to public disgrace.

The gravest and most dominant transgression today, as in the Days of Noah, is the complete absence of repentance. There was no remorse or regret that had begun with the pride of Cain; not even with the murder of his own brother, Abel. Cain's devilish prideful spirit had spread like a pandemic and swallowed up the multitudes of people in his generation. Cain and the fallen Watchers conspired to set the stage for godless empires to follow. By the time Noah came along, every imagination of Cain's heart was bestowed as a curse on all the impending generations. From the core of his sin was his prideful heart and the refusal to repent which was inherited from his true father, the devil.

Today, we have also betrayed our foundation of faith through repentance, just as in the Days of Noah. The gate of the repentant heart is the only avenue that God can move through. This spirit which is actively at work in the children of disobedience has built strongholds that have fortified the masses behind walls of unbelief that have abandoned the faith. The thirst for truth has been replaced with the thirst for sensual desire. The hunger for God's Word has been replaced with the hunger for the lies of social media and entertainment, even in the nominal church. Our eyes have been blinded by the glamour and glitz, to be ruled by our senses and the entrenching systematized error.

Contrary to most understanding, repentance is not about penance. Penance is the self-inflicted suffering, punishing someone from guilt, not conviction. This will never change your character or your conduct. Repentance is the doorway, not the destination to experiencing daily salvation. It is not the token act of baptism. As Christians, we must understand that the whole life of the Christian must be founded by unceasing prayer encircled by unceasing repentance. Jesus began his ministry with such a call: "Repent, for the kingdom of heaven is near." This is embracing His Lordship.

Our global secular society has done everything to erase Biblical truth and belief from education, government, and every facet of culture, only to replace it with foolish arrogance, and ignorance. This is a quote from Faisal Saeed Al Muter, who is the founder of the Global Secular Humanist Movement: "I think there have been many definitions proposed to identify what secular humanism actually means; they all go back to the same principles that we, as a species, can have fully ethical lives relying on ourselves using reason and science to solve problems without the belief in the supernatural. This is the perfect definition of what we are now drowning in.

It is very ironic that another quote that goes everywhere is based on the initials for the rock band, KISS. The quote "Keep it simple, stupid" is a design principle that states that simplicity is key to user acceptance and interaction. Kiss became one of America's most successful rock bands and a pop culture phenomenon in their Halowwen costumes. They built on the rebellion of the "Sixties."

Even a greater satire is this quote reflects the Apostle Paul's rebuke to the childish shurch in Corinth. Paul pled, "For I am jealous for you with godly jealousy. For I have betrothed you to one husband, that I may present *you as* a chaste virgin to Christ. But I fear, lest somehow, as the serpent deceived Eve by his craftiness, so your minds may be corrupted from the simplicity that is in Christ." We have followed suit leading our children.

Will You Be a Voice in the Wilderness?

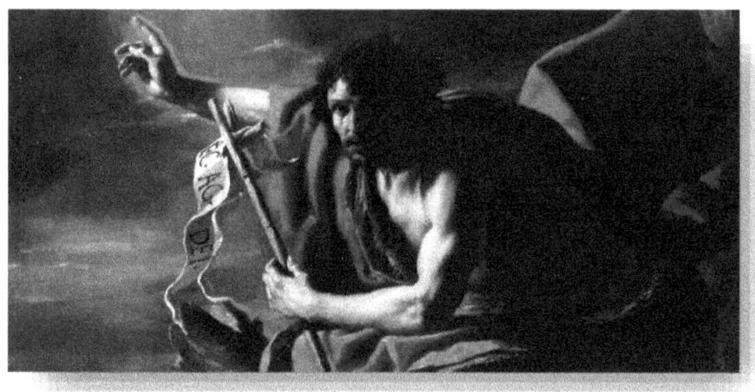

John 3

But when he saw many of the Pharisees and Sadducees coming to where he was baptizing, he said to them: "You brood of vipers! Who warned you to flee from the coming wrath? Produce fruit in keeping with repentance. And do not think you can say to yourselves, 'We have Abraham as our father.' I tell you that out of these stones God can raise up children for Abraham. The ax is already at the root of the trees, and every tree that does not produce good fruit will be cut down and thrown into the fire.

Except for the Lord Jesus Himself, no person had a greater calling than John the Baptist. He incapsulated every aspect of what God is calling for from this present generation. His pedigree was more than just natural. His formative years were also spent being raised in the Judaean desert, where the monastic Essenes dwelt. He grew up isolated from the ritual and the corruption from the merchandising in Jerusalem. John was raised up from the four hundred years of silence to begin the provocation of an unrepentant Israel. God began to break the mold of dead ritual and arrogant entitlement, laing the ax to the roots of a hypocritical religious regime. As John was exposed to the obscurity in the desert, eating wild locusts and honey as a radical prophet in camel's hair, John came out as a voice in the wilderness, crying out for repentance to prepare the way for the coming Messiah, who they would also reject.

John was the premier end-times prophet, not only opening the door to the Messiah, but His new covenant that would be written in His blood. He conducted his ministry with a prophetic authority that demanded immediate repentance. He taught that judgment was truly at hand, and it will thoroughly sift the threshing floor of Israel. This described the Messianic mission that the Pharisees and Sadducees were blinded by.

This began the cosmic war where Jesus warned them, "And from the days of John the Baptist until the present time, the kingdom of heaven has endured violent assault, yet violent men will seize it by force. Jesus' reference to violence referred to both the intensity of spiritual warfare surrounding the ministry of Jesus and His mission, and also to the intensity required to persevere in following God at all cost. Jesus had declared John the Baptizer as the greatest prophet, but that he would be the least in the kingdom of God. This appeared as a paradox, but it spoke to the future of the coming kingdom of the perpetual remnant being razed through the cross, beginning with His disciples.

Jesus the Messiah is now crying out to this generation as in the days of Noah to repent and take the mantle to be the John the Baptist generation that He is returning to. As the nominal church is caught in the same ritualistic theater and blessing with a kiss as the merchandising pharisees, the remnant is being called out to come out suffering the reproach of truth that Jesus demanded in the Book of Hebrews. I have already suffered reproach from the message entailed in the Exodus Trilogy. It is a declaration of the same war that called out John the Baptizer.

We are now experiencing what the faithful Nehemiah did where he found the cratered walls of Jerusalem with no place to blow the trumpet. He learned as a warrior to rebuild with a trough in one hand and a sword in the other. Only a warring remnant understands how critical of who is at the door. For the love of God, please do not miss your calling. Apathy and fear will take your crown if you let them. As the door to this generation is beginning to close, what side of the door are you on? The heartbreaking truth is, will this be known as the John the Baptist generation or the Judas generation?

The Coming Final Harvest

Revelation 14

I looked, and there before me was a white cloud, and seated on the cloud was one like a son of man with a crown of gold on his head and a sharp sickle in his hand. a sharp sickle in his hand.

The time of the last days harvest is certainly upon us. We must look up and realize that our Redeemer is knocking at the door with His blade as the spiritual waters are raging. This final church age represents the Laodicean church that forgot how to battle as they lost their "first love." We have to learn from history if we are to revive. My prayer is that the apathy and compromise will be consumed through true sifting revival by the conviction of our heavenly Shepherd. We do not need a renewal of legalism or another counterfeit revival. What we need is a rekindled passion for God and a vision of those perishing in the flames of deception and sensuality in this final rebellion.

All the disciples embraced their death at their martyrdom, except John who was boiled in oil and carried on that we might have the Book of Revelation. There is so much at stake as this generation fades away, living for the moment. We must empty our hearts of vain deception to receive a heart of conviction to find God's perfect will. We must embrace our Savior's cross and repel the adultery of this fallen world.

The foundational resistance to the present great rebellion that we are submerged in is a believing, abiding faith. It saved Noah and it will save us if we repent daily. It is not a one-time "get out of hell free card." It is radically holding on to Jesus that will keep the stain of this evil age from crippling us. We must trust in our commitment and hope in his Word and Spirit so we instantly discern the counterfeit. This will bring a harvest of joy and peace. The gathering of things planted in a natural time of reaping in joy, produces God's greatest blessing. Jesus reflected on the harvest when he enjoins believers to ask the "Lord of the harvest" for laborers.

The Grecian army of Alexander the Great gave a profound example of the power of commitment from their brutal war machine. They understood the power of commitment. At the prelude to war, the army of Greece was under equipped and outnumbered by their opponent. Alexander called the opposing general forward and asked him if he was ready to surrender. The general responded with laughter and great disdain because it was obvious that he had nothing to fear because they were a far greater force. Alexander turned to his first ten men and asked them to march. They marched directly over the cliff before them plundering to their death. Alexander assured the general that all his men were of the same character and conviction. The general was terrified, and surrendered immediately.

This generation has assured itself that it will never account for the way they live, but nothing could be further from the truth. Paul assured Timothy with the scripture, "Therefore, God exalted him to the highest place and gave him the name that is above every name, that at the name of Jesus every knee should bow, in heaven and on earth and under the earth, and every tongue acknowledge that Jesus Christ is Lord, to the glory of God the Father. This is why the reverent fear of God is the beginning of wisdom. It is bewildering how the Lordship of Christ is neglected when the earth despairs for the testimony of Christ. Alexander Hamilton warned, "Those who stand for nothing, fall for anything." Do we truly reflect who is your Lord is and what you believe?

The Beautiful Coming Sea of Glass

Revelation 15

And I saw what looked like a sea of glass glowing with fire and, standing beside the sea, those true believers who had been victorious over the beast and its image and over the number of its name.

The Apostle John saw something that was impossible to describe, because it was so different from anything he had ever seen. He witnessed a "Sea of Glass" that was an incredible, moving force, but the glass gave the impression of stillness like the waters in Psalm 23. How could a sea be made of glass? John was trying to convey the beautiful brilliant transparency, the vast expanse, and the deep purity of what he witnessed by the astonishing marriage of water and fire. It was eternity mingled with fire, representing the transformation of the ones standing upon it who had been fully refined by the Lord's testing. John had learned to envision through the eyes of Christ Jesus. Human perception is often too confined to comprehend the realities in the spiritual realm. For now, as Paul reflected that we see "through a glass darkly" we are haunted by the eyeglass of carnality, that blinds us from the heavenly realities that will remain mysteries, until we see them for ourselves with glorified eyes and the mind of Christ.

The assault of this world, our flesh and the devil always take its toll, but it is engraving our soul for eternity's mission. But when our heavenly calling s arrived, our first glance behind us is to see the perilous dangers that we have escaped. It will imprint upon us a far greater impact than the entire road of discipline through which was the valley that we had journeyed. For we shall then see our horrific accumulation of sin, understand how appalling it was, and be dazzled with amazement at the love which He bore for us while we went on day, after day repeating and multiplying transgressions, calloused by this present evil age.

As we turn away from this dark and painful day of battle, we will be emptied at last of our pride and our selfish will. If we find our knees in repentance, we will be over-powered with humble gratitude, crying aloud, with love and devotion unrecognized by this world. The entire book speaks to the futility of the carnal life. Without God and without eternal purpose we will all fall short of God's glory. The second is that "the wounds of a friend are better than the kisses of an enemy." If we respond, all of our tears will soon be wiped away as He promised, as we enter eternal bliss of full sonship.

May we all learn to answer God's call to repentance and truly believe in this great hour of testing.

Come Lord Jesus!

The Second Book of the Trilogy

In the Valley of Decision

This is a riveting book about the loss of our Christian heritage and our superpower status in the world. It explains why our planet is reeling toward Armageddon from Wall Street to the Middle East. It is an answer to some sobering questions about the near future.

Who is Babylon the Great in the last days?

Are we "One nation under God" or one nation under the judgment of God?

The Third Book of the Trilogy

The Sifting Blade of the Messiah is the last book summarizing the Exodus Trilogy that exposes the Global Reset, the apostate church and the rescue of the remnant from the Two Corporate Witnesses of God's eternal purpose. This may be the book that I wish that I had never wrote. It is the exposure of our Messiah's final acts of the final hour on planet earth and the final betrayal of our precious Messiah.